T0323895

Alliance Contracting in Health and Social Care

Alliance Contracting in Health and Social Care is a ground-breaking and practical guide to collaborating and co-ordinating service provision across different providers, taking readers through each step from initial concept to launch and operation.

Responding to the need for more joined up services, the book explains how alliancing and alliance contracting can tackle the system issues which often stymie collaboration between different agencies. It takes a people-centred approach providing guidance for the legal, financial and governance frameworks needed for organisations to work together, ultimately providing better health and social care. Written by a leading expert in the field, it also features detailed examples of where alliancing has already proved successful, including services around mental health and homelessness in different regions of the UK.

This important book will be essential reading for anyone commissioning services across the health and social care sector, in both the UK and beyond.

Linda Hutchinson is a leading expert on alliance contracts as applied to the public sector. She is a highly experienced facilitator of successful interprofessional and interorganisational collaborations in a wide range of health and care services.

Alliance Contracting in Health and Social Care

A Practical Guide to Commissioning for Collaboration

Linda Hutchinson

Routledge
Taylor & Francis Group

LONDON AND NEW YORK

Designed cover image: © Central Station Design

First published 2025
by Routledge
4 Park Square, Milton Park, Abingdon, Oxon OX14 4RN

and by Routledge
605 Third Avenue, New York, NY 10158

Routledge is an imprint of the Taylor & Francis Group, an informa business

© 2025 Linda Hutchinson

The right of Linda Hutchinson to be identified as author of this work has been asserted in accordance with sections 77 and 78 of the Copyright, Designs and Patents Act 1988.

British Library Cataloguing-in-Publication Data
A catalogue record for this book is available from the British Library

ISBN: 978-1-032-84231-8 (hbk)
ISBN: 978-1-032-83474-0 (pbk)
ISBN: 978-1-003-51180-9 (ebk)

DOI: 10.4324/9781003511809

Typeset in Times New Roman
by Apex CoVantage, LLC

To the two Andrews: my brother for his wisdom, generosity and guidance; and my husband for everything and more.

Contents

About the author

Linda Hutchinson is a Director of Ideas Alliance CIC, a social enterprise consultancy specialising in collaboration and co-production. Linda has advised on and facilitated the development of alliances and other collaborations with a wide range of commissioner and provider organisations in health, the justice sector, youth unemployment, domestic violence and care services.

Previously, Linda was a paediatric consultant in London, and held Director-level posts in hospitals and health and care regulators. Her frontline experience and senior executive roles in the UK National Health Service (NHS) and other national bodies means she is fully conversant with the policy, regulatory and operational realities of effecting change in the public sector.

Case studies

Preface

I was sitting in my brother Andrew's kitchen in Melbourne, Australia, in 2005. He was telling me about his work getting oil, construction and utility companies to work together for the best outcomes rather than only for the money. I was intrigued. How had they managed to get collaboration and innovation in such commercial and competitive environments? If they could do that, surely we can do it in health and care.

Andrew told me more. They used a technique called 'alliance contracting', where everyone is signed up to one contract and shares responsibility for the whole project, rather than each party only contracted for the services they provide. This simple change shifts mindsets and drives collaboration and innovation.

I was working at the time in national policy in what was to become NHS England, so was aware of the developments in commissioning, contracting and financing of the NHS. As a paediatrician I was already used to working with others outside health – in schools, child protection, local communities, the police. There is also a strong network of general paediatricians and specialists with mutual respect and assistance, all seeking to do the best for children and their families.

I know most people have a strong desire to work together and learn from each other. In health and care we are motivated by a commitment to do the right thing and help where it is needed. However, there is a lot that can get in the way – from heavy workloads preventing the space for thinking or meeting together, through to differences in remuneration or structural barriers to sharing ideas and responsibilities. It was not unusual to hear comments like: 'We can't do that as it is not in our contract.'

In Australia, Andrew and I talked further about alliancing and alliance contracting. I kept asking him more and more questions, and he generously gave me his time and expertise. On returning to the UK, I was caught up in my job and, later, a move to help set up the Care Quality Commission (CQC). It wasn't until 2011 that I had the opportunity to see whether there was any scope for applying alliance contracting in the UK.

Awareness of different ways of commissioning services in health and care was growing in the late 2000s. When I talked to people about an established methodology that drove collaboration and innovation, there was considerable interest. However, it had not been tried in health and care, so we had to carefully think through how to adopt and adapt.

Denis O'Rourke from Lambeth Council (London) and Nick Dixon from Stockport Council (Greater Manchester) were the brave commissioners who took the first steps and set up alliance contracts in 2012/13. I was also lucky to connect with Robert Breedon, a lawyer from Wragge & Co (now Gowling WLG), who was also looking at alliance contracting. His firm had developed alliance contracts in defence and Robert, who worked in the healthcare arm at the time, thought the method would be applicable there too. He brought the legal expertise and much-needed reassurance to our early work.

Now, over 12 years later, we have a range of health and care alliances up and running, and more in development. There has been a lot of learning and a wealth of experience. This book is my attempt to write that all down. It covers all aspects of alliances, from the pre-development stage right through to launch and the years of operation. I use real examples and don't shy away from saying where we got things wrong or might have done things differently. I've also included some of the materials my brother kindly shared with me in the first place, even though we have not always been able to put all their best practice into use.

This book is for those interested in collaboration in health and social care, but many of the concepts and principles apply to any form of partnership and to any sector. I hope you will read the book and be able to apply its guidance to your own context, and maybe develop the ideas even further.

About this book

The book is based around our four-step approach to alliance development, which reflects many years' experience of alliancing in different sectors and 12 years of application to UK public services. In practice, of course, the steps

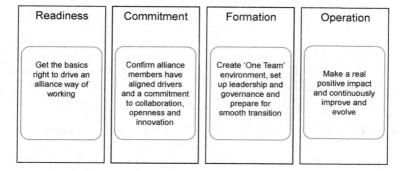

Readiness	Commitment	Formation	Operation
Get the basics right to drive an alliance way of working	Confirm alliance members have aligned drivers and a commitment to collaboration, openness and innovation	Create 'One Team' environment, set up leadership and governance and prepare for smooth transition	Make a real positive impact and continuously improve and evolve

Figure 0a.1 Four steps to creating successful alliances

do not run in neat chronological order. However, they act as a framework where all the different aspects of alliance development and maintenance are covered.

The 'Readiness' step, all about getting the basics right, allows you to look at your alliance's development from several angles. It means you will have considered a whole range of issues and been able to get approval from your organisation to move ahead.

The next step, which we have called 'Commitment', is about getting the right members on board and everyone committed to the alliance way of working. This means all parties can confidently sign the legal agreement.

You are then into the alliance itself and, in the 'Formation' step, we cover the leadership and governance you will need as well as the alliance culture. Some of this you will have started right at the beginning and other aspects will need attention in the early days of the alliance.

The 'Operation' step is about the steady state of your alliance and how you can maximise impact and create a constantly improving high-performance alliance.

Each step is broken down into two components, and there is a chapter explaining each one. At the end of each chapter, I give a case study of one of the alliances, presented in chronological order of their start dates. The information in the case studies and the real examples throughout the book are based on my time working closely with developing and new alliances. More recently I have spoken to people who remain involved in their alliances to hear about their progress and any comments and insights. I am grateful to everyone for sharing their time and their thoughts. Any inaccuracies or misinterpretations as I translated these to the text are my own.

In writing the book, I found it easiest to replicate the way I work as an alliance facilitator. I usually work initially with people from a public sector

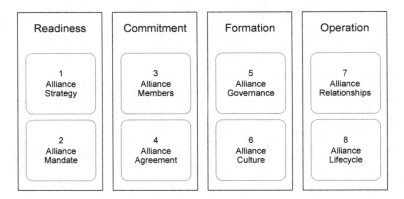

Readiness	Commitment	Formation	Operation
1 Alliance Strategy	3 Alliance Members	5 Alliance Governance	7 Alliance Relationships
2 Alliance Mandate	4 Alliance Agreement	6 Alliance Culture	8 Alliance Lifecycle

Figure 0a.2 Four steps and book chapters

commissioning organisation who are planning to set up an alliance, so when the text in those chapters refers to 'you', that is who I have in mind. Where I am referring to 'you' as someone from a delivery organisation contemplating joining an alliance, I make that clear.

Once alliances are formed, I work alongside the whole alliance and all the members. In later chapters, the 'you' is therefore any member of an alliance.

I hope this approach makes sense, even for those of you who are none of the above. My intention is to make it feel as real and practical as possible, whether you read the book from start to finish or dip in and out as your own alliance develops.

Introduction to alliances

There are many forms of collaboration and many uses of the word 'alliance'. This book is specifically about alliance contracting, a fully integrated risk- and responsibility-sharing form of collaboration. Before we get into detail it is helpful to clarify some terms and, importantly, what we mean by alliances in this book. We will also talk generally about alliance contracts and some of their key components.

Spectrum of collaboration

When people tell me they are involved in a partnership, alliance or consortium, I've learnt to ask a few questions so that I can understand the nature of their collaboration rather than rely on the words they use. The same word can mean different things to different people. To help with this, I started to use the idea of a 'spectrum of collaboration'. I'll explain the words I use and what I mean by them.

Informal collaboration

At one end there are informal collaborations that happen all the time in our working and personal life. People come together because they have something in common, a shared interest. These are great ways to build relationships and swap ideas. They can be inclusive, open invitation and involve a large number of people. The informality and openness are important. Any ideas that are shared may lead to changes in how some people work, but there are unlikely to be any major changes to core business or implementation of significant development or change. This is not what these informal collaborations are about.

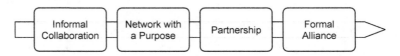

Figure 0b.1 Spectrum of collaboration

Network with a purpose

Next along the spectrum is what I call 'Network with a Purpose', where a group of people come together for a specific reason. It may be a team put together for a few months, or a new committee or group to tackle a specific issue. These are very common in my old world of the NHS. There may be dedicated funding, either externally granted or developed by members of the network by pooling funds.

Again, these are good for relationship building, and may result in people working differently for a while. There may even be some sharing of resources and people to get the task done. However there is still unlikely to be lasting change to working practices, and the activity is usually seen as an 'add-on' to normal business rather than the 'day job'.

Partnerships

We then start to get into partnerships. These can range from strategic relationships – where, for example, organisations bid together for funding – through to shared responsibility for manufacture or delivery. To be honest, you would probably need a spectrum of partnerships to capture the huge range of what people might include here. At the far end, some may be very similar to alliances.

When people ask me what the difference is between a partnership and our type of alliance I usually say that an alliance is like a supercharged partnership. In most partnerships you see arrangements where each party carries out its share of the work and people come together monthly or at other intervals to talk about how they are getting on. There may be some joint reporting or other collective working, but not always. In the alliances we set up, everything is a shared endeavour.

Formal alliances

Moving on to formal alliances, again there can be a wide range of types of collaboration that use the term 'alliance'. There can be large international alliances such as GAVI (the Global Alliance for Vaccines and Immunization), business-to-business alliances (as in the Star Alliance in the airline industry) or multi-organisation alliances for provision such as cancer services in a particular area. Alliancing can be applied to delivery of services, co-design, research and development, innovation and change programmes.

If you look up the word 'alliance' in a dictionary, you'll find something like: 'an agreement between two or more individuals or entities stating that the involved parties will act in a certain way in order to achieve a common goal'. The nature of the agreement reflects the nature of the alliance. It can be a simple statement about its purpose, outcomes expected and the roles and accountabilities of its members. It could be a Memorandum of Understanding or similar, or it could be a legal deed, as in our alliances.

The alliances in this book are intense collaborations where there is full sharing of responsibilities and risks. Everyone is responsible for everything, not just their own area of expertise or delivery. Members of the Alliance plan together, make the big decisions together and help each other out. In essence, they will all succeed or fail together. That may sound scary, but it is the magic ingredient that leads to transformation and success.

However, a note of caution: alliance contracts are not good for large groups. This is a practical issue about how many people are involved in the big decisions, especially financial ones, and the need for unanimity. Once you start getting more than eight members, it is harder to do this.

Also, an alliance is not good for organisations that are not aligned with its purpose. We'll talk about this later; but, for now, note that, if any member of the Alliance will be worse off if the Alliance is successful – for instance, less financially stable, subject to a change of activity so it is no longer able to fulfil its own constitution, facing significant workforce reductions and income – then their ability to be a committed member of the Alliance will be constrained, if not impossible. This is true for all collaborations, and the reason many fail to achieve their aims. Checking for and being honest about misalignments is therefore vital before entering a risk-sharing alliance.

In summary, there are many different ways to collaborate, and the type of collaboration needs to be right for the circumstances. As you think about your collaboration, you can recognise where it sits on the spectrum. If you were to move it to a more formal arrangement, it is good to consider not only what you will gain but also what you might lose.

Our alliances are formal, legally defined collaborations, and that is what we will be talking about in the remainder of the book.

The history of alliance contracting

Alliance contracting for delivering projects has grown rapidly since it was first adopted with outstanding results in the early 1990s for the development of oil fields in the North Sea. It has since been used in thousands of projects, and continues to produce outstanding cost outcomes, early completion, exemplary health and safety records and award-winning solutions.

The first alliance contract in the oil industry

Alliance contracting grew out of frustration in the oil industry. Every new oil platform built in the North Sea in the 1980s ended up running late, with escalating costs and often with the financiers, contractors, designers and suppliers suing and countersuing each other for years after.

The contracts in use at the time were traditional service contracts with each individual party, each with its own specifications, performance indicators, incentives and penalties. Contracts got longer and longer with each new project as the lawyers tried to anticipate and specify every eventuality. People tried different ways to manage projects, such as having lead contractors, but the problems remained.

A few individuals decided to approach contracting in a completely different way, and created what was to become the first alliance contract. The results were impressive. When the first oil rig was built under this method the usual cost of a new platform was around £450 million. When the alliance came together, the members collectively estimated the target cost to be £383 million. They revised this down further after a few months, and in fact the final cost was £290 million – 35 per cent lower than the market norm of the time. On top of this, the rig was completed six months ahead of schedule (Sakal, 2005).

After this, alliance contracting became established, particularly in Australia and New Zealand, where it is known as 'project alliancing'. In the mid-1990s, Australia hosted the first civil construction project using such alliancing, followed by the first public sector one in 1998.

Alliancing in the health and care context

The health and care sector is, of course, very different to the oil industry. The UK has the government-funded National Health Service (NHS) for all citizens. NHS hospitals and many of the delivery organisations are public bodies; and general practices – general practitioner (GP/family doctor services) – while run as separate entities, are wholly or mainly funded through public money.

The care sector, by contrast, depends on individual private, charitable or voluntary sector organisations for much of the delivery. Local authorities and other public sector bodies are responsible for ensuring services are available for their populations. They receive central government funding for this as well as having the ability to generate income directly.

Trends and changes in commissioning public services

In the past many care services would have been provided directly by local authorities. Starting in about the mid-1980s, there was a move to outsource delivery. The concept of operating public services through competitive procurement and contract management took off.

Similarly, in the NHS in England, an 'internal market' was created in the early 1990s when, on the premise that competition for resources would create efficiency and innovation, purchasing services was separated out from delivery (Wenzel et al., 2023). Organisations to carry out the commissioning were created, and have undergone reform and reorganisation multiple times since then.

More recently there has been recognition of market limitations in health and care. The overall direction in the 2010s saw a desire to move away from a transactional, contract management approach that focuses on data and performance metrics. These do not sit well with human services and interactions full of connection and emotion. They also do not foster partnership working and integrated care.

Suffice to say we have started to move from a paradigm predicated on competition to drive efficiency and contract management to ensure value for money to one that recognises inherent complexity and multiple stakeholder perspectives.

Movements such as Human Learning Systems (n.d.) and Community Wealth Building (Centre for Local Economic Strategies, n.d.) are helping to challenge the accepted ways of working, and providing examples of putting values and people front and centre. This has led to increasing numbers of people who have witnessed the benefits of new ways of working.

Recent developments in UK health and care

While wholesale change has not yet happened, there are encouraging signs at the macro level. The NHS in England is now arranged into 42 Integrated Care Systems (ICSs), recognising the importance of collaboration and integration across multiple parties. The NHS, councils, the voluntary sector and other partners share the development of plans to improve health and care services, with a focus on prevention, better outcomes and reducing health inequalities (NHS England, n.d.).

In Scotland, the same move towards integration has come about with the creation of 31 Health and Social Care Partnerships from the previous NHS Boards and local authorities. These integrated authorities manage the funding for health and social care for their populations (Scottish Government, n.d.).

Similar arrangements exist in Northern Ireland, where six Health and Social Care Trusts have responsibility for the management and administration of regional health and social care facilities and services (NI Direct Government Services, n.d.).

In Wales, seven local Health Boards bring together the planning and delivery of primary, community and secondary healthcare services alongside specialist services for their areas. They are also responsible for providing services in partnership, improving physical and mental health outcomes, promoting wellbeing and reducing health inequalities across their population (NHS Confederation, 2021). Social care responsibilities sit with local authorities that work closely with the Health Boards.

In addition, there are Regional Partnership Boards that operate on the same footprints as the seven Health Boards (Welsh Government, 2022). These bring together other health boards and local authorities, along with citizens, carers, providers and the charitable and voluntary sector, to meet the care and support needs of local people.

The missing link

Bringing organisations together for strategic development and the potential to pool funding creates the context for permission for, and even expectation of, joined-up thinking at the level of the individual accessing support or care. However, this won't necessarily make that happen.

Similarly, you can support the move to shared purpose, shared values and a focus on learning and relationships; but when you have large amounts of public money in play, with the political and media scrutiny that goes with it, you need something more.

This is where alliancing and alliancing contracting comes in. In essence, alliance contracting bridges the gap between the desire for collaboration and putting people first with the legal, governance and financial assurance needed when public money is involved.

For me, this was the missing element. I had seen many good, well-planned transformation programmes fail to deliver or spread as people tried to make them work in a financial and governance system that supports silos and self-interest. It is a question of tackling both: keeping the innate enthusiasm for working collaboratively that is always there with people in the public sector and not-for-profit world; and creating shared financial and legal responsibility that is transparent and appropriate for publicly financed services.

Spreading the word

In the early 2010s, the incoming coalition government was planning to embed commissioning decision making by clinical professionals in the English NHS, through Clinical Commissioning Groups at local borough or county level. This led to an evolution of commissioning over the next decade, as documented by Allen et al. (2020). This reorganisation was an opportunity to talk to people who were new to such roles about different ways to commission. For me, the issue is not who does the commissioning, but how it is done.

Another factor helping to spread the word was the Canterbury Clinical Network (CCN) health system alliance, which was launched in New Zealand around 2008/2009 and discontinued in 2024. Although not an alliance contract, it was influenced by the methodology, and many of the core elements are similar. The Network was later instrumental in the rapid and effective health service response to the 2011 earthquake. The London-based

King's Fund took a keen interest in the CCN model, and published a number of reports on it (Timmins, 2013). The widespread interest in and publicity surrounding the New Zealand approach helped make 'alliancing' a familiar term in the UK.

Our first alliance contract was in 2012 in Stockport. It was very small in value and did not have the full spectrum of features, but it was a start and the learning began. Soon to follow was the alliance in mental health services in the London borough of Lambeth (see Case Study 1).

Shortly after this, the Mid-Notts Better Together Alliance was created, influenced in part by the New Zealand model as well as an integrated care initiative in Spain. Better Together was a large strategic alliance with multiple member organisations. It involved the Clinical Commissioning Group, the local authority, two NHS Trusts, a GP collaborative and a voluntary sector organisation, and covered all health and social services for all ages. Better Together used the Alliance Principles and had other similarities with the alliances described in this book. It was an overarching collaboration with the existing structural base remaining as before. There was limited shared financial responsibility and no legally binding agreement. It was successful in bringing people together, developing relationships and creating a collaborative environment that led to smaller specific joint projects and developments (see Case Study 5).

Those involved in the Nottinghamshire Alliance now talk about how their experience created the context for other specific joint projects and developments. In addition, its high profile and recognition and permission to create it from NHS England established alliance contracting as an accepted approach.

Alliance contracting – an overview

Whenever I talk about the specifics of alliance contracting, I always start by emphasising that it is first and foremost a way of working based on trust, relationships and shared purpose. It is important to recognise that contracts and legal agreements support or accelerate collaboration; they cannot, by themselves, create it.

High levels of trust and strong relationships are needed for all successful collaborations. These are not unique to alliance contracts of course. Alliance contracting extends the level of collaboration to shared financial and operational responsibility. This is the step that really changes behaviours. You can do a lot working with others; but when you truly share overall financial and operational responsibility and risk and make decisions together on these, you get a completely different level of collaboration and innovation. This makes the need for trust and strong relationships even more important.

The benefits of alliances come from the strong foundation of collaborative decision making, with clarity about common goals and collective commitment to achieving them. There is team and individual accountability within an appropriate governance and management structure. With these factors in place and a high trust environment the following are enabled:

- collective ownership, responsibility and accountability
- collective response to external influences and risk
- optimal decision making
- pooling of skills, assets and experience
- hard conversations and working through potential conflict
- flexibility to evolve over time.

One contract, one definition of success

An alliance contract is a single agreement between the owner (financier, commissioner) and the parties delivering a service or project (providers). This differs from traditional contracts, where there are separate contracts with each party, with different objectives, performance measures and incentives. By having one contract, all parties are working to the same objectives and are signed up to the same definition of success.

Alliance contracts create collaborative environments without the need for new organisational forms. Parties to the contract come together to deliver the objectives or outcomes, those that matter to people who use the services or support. Having one overall performance framework means that each party has a stake in the success of the others. There is thus a strong sense of 'Your problem is my problem, your success is my success.'

Collective ownership and responsibility

What makes an alliance contract different is risk management. In traditional contracts the risks are allocated by the owner to the party deemed most able to

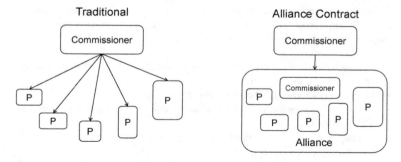

P = provider organisation

Figure 0b.2 Traditional versus alliance contracting

manage them. In an alliance, however, there is a collective ownership of risks, opportunities and responsibilities associated with delivery of the whole project.

There are no longer one-to-one discussions with the funder or commissioner where different providers might push their own agenda regardless of others. An alliance contract means being part of a whole; all partners need to talk about how to move forward. Any 'gain' or 'pain' is linked with good or poor outcomes overall, and not to the performance of individual parties.

Another main difference is in the focus on relationships rather than transactions, with the concept of collective responsibility key. Once the contract is in place, the participants work as a fully integrated team throughout implementation.

In sum, an alliance contract means no more 'us' and 'them'. It is now 'we', and we are all judged on how we all act and deliver together.

Outcome-based to drive innovation and change

An alliance contract is outcome-based; it does not prescribe a detailed service specification. There is an assumption that the service model at the end of the contract term should be different to that at the start as there will be constant improvement; therefore it makes no sense to describe it in the legal document. Details of service delivery and operational plans are required of course, but in documents owned by the alliance and constantly reviewed and updated.

Being a member of an alliance means being focused on delivering the outcomes for those you serve and making a commitment to change and adapt as you go along to make that happen.

Commitment to Alliance Principles

The Alliance Principles describe the commitment everyone makes to behaving 'in a certain way' to achieve the common goal. They are applicable to any form of collaboration, but are essential for financial and risk-sharing ones. A full description of and rationale for all the principles is given in Chapter 2; but, briefly, they require all parties to an agreement:

- to assume collective responsibility for all the risks involved in providing services under the agreement;
- to make decisions on a 'best for people using services' basis;
- to commit to unanimous, principle- and value-based decision making on all key issues;
- to adopt a culture of 'no fault, no blame' among participants and seek to avoid all disputes and litigation;
- to adopt open-book accounting and transparency in all matters;
- to appoint and allocate key roles on a best person basis; and
- to act in accordance with the Alliance values and behaviours at all times.

The Alliance Principles are non-negotiable as they are necessary for creating the high levels of trust and strong relationships that allow true collaborative risk and responsibility sharing.

Summary

As we end this introduction, you should have a clear sense of the type of alliance we are talking about in this book. It is not an informal collaboration or a business-to-business alliance; it is a full risk- and responsibility-sharing contractual relationship between one or more commissioners of public services and a number of provider organisations.

In the next chapter we will start at the beginning of the process of developing an alliance: what needs to be considered and in place to make the development of an alliance possible, practical and successful.

References

Allen, P., Checkland, K., Moran, V., & Peckham, S. (Eds.) (2020). *Commissioning healthcare in England: Evidence, policy and practice*. Policy Press.

Centre for Economic Local Strategies. (n.d.). *What is community wealth building?* Retrieved 15 March 2024 from https://cles.org.uk/community-wealth-building/what-is-community-wealth-building/.

NHS Confederation. (2021, May 21). *About the NHS in Wales*. https://nhsconfed.org/articles/about-nhs-wales.

NHS England. (n.d.). *What are integrated care systems?* Retrieved 14 March 2024 from https://www.england.nhs.uk/integratedcare/what-is-integrated-care/.

NI Direct Government Services/té díreach seirbhísí rialtais (n.d.). *Health and social care trusts*. Retrieved 14 March 2024 from https://www.nidirect.gov.uk/contacts/health-and-social-care-trusts.

Sakal, M.W. (2005). Project alliancing: A relational contracting mechanism for dynamic projects. *Lean Construction Journal*, 2(1), 67–79. https://doi.org/10.60164/b5h4e3h6e/.

Scottish Government/Riaghaltas na h-Alba. (n.d.). *Health and social care integration*. Retrieved 14 March 2024 from https://www.gov.scot/policies/social-care/health-and-social-care-integration/.

Timmins, N. (2013, September 11). *Canterbury, New Zealand's quest for integrated care*. The King's Fund. https://www.kingsfund.org.uk/insight-and-analysis/videos/nicholas-timmins-canterbury-new-zealands-quest-integrated-care.

Welsh Government/Llwodraeth Cymru. (2022, September 14). *Regional Partnership Boards (RPBs)*. https://www.gov.wales/regional-partnership-boards-rpbs.

Wenzel, L., Robertson, R., & Wickens, C. (2023, July 20). *What is commissioning and how is it changing?* The King's Fund. https://www.kingsfund.org.uk/insight-and-analysis/long-reads/what-commissioning-and-how-it-changing.

Case study 1

Lambeth – Integrated Personalised Support Alliance (2015–2018)

Lambeth's Integrated Personalised Support Alliance (IPSA) provided support and services for people with severe and enduring mental illness. The overall aim was to maximise their independence and participation, and enable them to recover and stay well. IPSA brought together four providers – a mental health trust, adult social care and two charities – and went live in April 2015 for a two-year period, extendable for one year. Its initial budget was £12 million a year, and it ran until July 2018, when it was included in Lambeth's new Living Well Network Alliance.

Creating the Alliance

An alliancing approach fitted with the ethos and values of the Lambeth Living Well (LLW) Collaborative. Set up in 2010, it brings together people using services, providers and commissioners to create ideas and plans for improving mental health services and support in the borough. New local initiatives were implemented; but, to move to the next level of transformation, Lambeth Clinical Commissioning Group (CCG) and Council felt that a formal change to contracting and financial arrangements was needed.

In early 2014, the commissioners therefore reviewed the best contracting and procurement approach for achieving their aims. Following an options appraisal, they selected an alliance contract. The CCG and Council then invited proposals from providers who had shown willingness to invest time and ideas to participate in the LLW Collaborative. The alliance members were confirmed in summer of that year and, together with the commissioners, formed the Integrated Personalised Support Alliance (IPSA).

Progress of the Alliance

IPSA established a new way of working, using an integrated team of voluntary sector staff, social workers, nurses, occupational therapists and consultant psychiatrists to intensively support people in their homes who would previously have been admitted to hospital. This, combined with a new intensive community rehabilitation service, reduced new admissions to hospital by 60 per cent in the first year.

For those who did require admission, IPSA offered various ways to ensure that housing and social connections ready for their discharge, and flexible ways to bridge hospital and community support. For those in residential care, a joint team with broad expertise meant that conversations could be had with people about moving to more independent and suitable premises.

IPSA was also able to create more accommodation – both self-contained and shared, and with or without integral support – from social housing providers, the open market and partner organisations. This led to increased choice and control of different types of places providing support.

What changed for people

IPSA was very successful in achieving its objectives of improving people's lives, reducing the need for residential placements and meeting financial challenges. By the end of the second year, of the 260 people in secure or highly specialised residential placements, 69 per cent moved into more suitable community-based accommodation and 19 per cent had a personal budget. The rate of new admissions to hospital or to specialised residential care dropped considerably. This enabled the initial budget of £12 million per annum to be reduced to £9.5 million, and an inpatient ward was closed.

The success of this alliance provided the confidence to go on to create the larger Living Well Network Alliance, which provides the majority of adult mental health services in the borough of Lambeth (see Case Study 4).

1   Alliance strategy

In this chapter we will be building your Alliance Strategy through a series of considerations about drivers for change and potential benefits and risks. We will look at a full contract options process that brings in others to make sure you have a well-rounded case that is inclusive and open. This will stand you in good stead for any challenges as you set up and run your alliance. We will also consider commissioner readiness, capability and capacity as these are critical for the success of your alliance development.

By the end of this chapter you should have all you need to be able to write a case for change, a business case or a strategy document for setting up an alliance.

Contracts and collaboration

When people hear about alliance contracting they are often enthused about the concept and can see many possibilities. After all, a methodology based on trust and relationships where the focus is on delivering for people feels like a no-brainer.

I have conducted many introductory sessions for local authorities, government departments and other commissioning organisations looking to change the way they commission. When they start to think through how they can move away from their existing ways of commissioning it can seem like there are a 101 things to consider.

We recommend breaking things down and considering, first, what type of collaboration is needed to achieve the goals. Alliances are one of many ways to collaborate. Whichever approach you take, it must be right for what you are aiming to achieve and the environment you are in. It is imperative to think about the collaboration first and then the method for achieving your aims, which might be through an alliance contract.

The remit for your collaboration

Many commissioners will have started describing the collaboration and its aims well before any consideration of commissioning method or contractual

DOI: 10.4324/9781003511809-1

form. Ideally, there will have been numerous conversations, inputs, ideas and insights from a range of people about support and services in the future. People with lived experiences and those who have drawn on support should be front and centre as their insights and revelations about what has gone before will provide rich material about what is good and should be built on and what needs to change.

Our experience is that this invariably makes for a more intense form of collaboration than has existed in the past. Better co-ordination, fewer referrals and handovers, less repetition of my story – all these commonly come from hearing about the reality on the ground. Your role is to turn all the information into the shared purpose for the alliance. We go into the detail of this in the next chapter, but for now you need a few parameters in order to consider how to best achieve it through your commissioning role.

Who is your collaboration for?

The first question to ask is who your collaboration is being set up for as we have some alliances for very specific groups and others for a wider population. For example, the first Lambeth Alliance was for a defined group of people with severe and enduring mental health disorders; and the second was for anyone aged 18–65 years in the borough with any mental health concerns (except for a few specific diagnoses) – two very different populations.

You may be tempted to define a set of people by age group, or by clinical or social description. Labels can be problematic and excluding, but are often inevitable at this stage. Ideally you should avoid labels becoming barriers to access with thresholds to be reached.

Alliance in practice – The Prevention Alliance (TPA)

In Stockport (Greater Manchester) there were multiple organisations contracted to deliver services. Some catered only for people who had had a stroke, for example; others were for individuals and family members living with dementia; and others for people in debt. While each of these organisations may have been excellent, there were the inevitable handovers as people went to the 'wrong' service or where people needed more than one source of support. Also, there may have been no joined-up thinking – for instance, with two neighbours being supported by different organisations for very similar reasons, but no one taking the initiative to connect them. The example often used was of two men who liked to play chess. One organisation arranged a volunteer to play with one man, and a second organisation arranged for another volunteer to play with the other. When it was suggested that the two men could play a game together, no one wanted to take responsibility to drive one to the other's house. They weren't 'allowed to' – so both men continued to 'get a service' each rather than receiving help to meet each other.

Stockport Council turned this situation on its head by setting up The Prevention Alliance to provide generic support and services to anyone, regardless of reason. If a person makes contact, someone will discuss with them any support and services they might choose – not dependent on a label or meeting specific criteria. The council also created the expectation of 'people helping people', rather than relying on services.

When deciding on the target group, check that it is realistic. There are always fuzzy edges. If the collaboration is for adults, what about young people in transition? If it is for residents, what about those outside the area but registered with a GP within it? These issues of scope are no different to any other form of contract. The key is to create flexibility and an expectation of pragmatism.

What will it do?

Now you can turn to the activities you want the collaboration to do. A common requirement is to set up a central co-ordination team and single points of access (virtual or otherwise). Is your collaboration going to deliver everything, or will it deliver some and co-ordinate the rest through subcontracts and partners? A helpful approach here is to fast-forward and imagine everything is up and running. Who is it for? Who will be making contact? What is happening? What is the alliance responsible for?

At this stage there will be some questions to be resolved about scope. This is normal and should not hold you up from describing your vision in enough detail to be able to proceed and test ideas.

Why choose an alliance?

Now you have confirmed what you want from the collaboration you are setting up, you can consider whether an alliance is a suitable vehicle. Alliances drive collaboration and innovation, which are often what commissioners are seeking when looking at different ways of working. It seems, therefore, that an alliance is a good approach.

However, an alliance will not be successful if it is the wrong choice. We'll go through the situations most suitable for alliances and some conditions that should make you think twice. It is important to understand upfront that alliances can be time-consuming to set up and run. They require people's time, energy and commitment. Where these may be in short supply, you may need to look for other ways to create a collaborative environment. In addition, alliances are risk-sharing contracts as opposed to risk-allocation ones. This means that they are not suitable for commissioners who prefer the language and behaviours of 'parent/child' contract relationships.

To help determine whether an alliance is the right approach for your context, a series of considerations are outlined here.

Knowns and unknowns

In some situations, there may be a high level of certainty about what is to be delivered, and this is unlikely to change much. The risks are minimal and can be clearly and separately allocated and managed. In that case, a services contract, based on risk allocation to the contracted party, should be perfectly suitable.

However, as Jim Ross – an engineer and management consultant who has been at the forefront of alliancing in Australia and around the world – summarised well in a paper prepared for an alliance master class in 2009, there are many situations where there are:

- numerous complex and/or unpredictable risks
- complex interfaces
- difficult stakeholder issues
- complex external threats
- very tight time frames
- high likelihood of scope/constraint change.
- a need for owner interference or significant value-adding input by the owner, or
- threats and/or opportunities that can only be managed collectively.

He explains that, if these criteria are present, then any attempt to allocate risk to different parties is likely to be illusionary and may give rise to conflict (Ross, 2009, p. 11). In these circumstances, success is more likely when all participants, owner and providers alike, assume collective responsibility for delivering the outcomes.

The Australia National Audit Office *Better practice guide* (2001) had a similar approach to contract management, albeit with reference to sectors such as energy, infrastructure and construction. It stated that alliance relationships are best suited for providing services that:

- That are difficult to define; or
- Are likely to change substantially over time; or
- Need innovative solutions from the providers; and
- Need creative management by the purchaser.

Many of these criteria apply in the public sector. Indeed, it is hard to think of any set of services and support where they do not apply. The bottom line is that you don't need an alliance if there is a lot of certainty or little need for change. Where there is uncertainty, expected or necessary changes to be made or a range of key parties, an alliance is a good choice.

Strengths-based and personalised

Some of the uncertainty mentioned above may be exactly what you want. There is increasing recognition that we should work alongside people to understand what matters to them and what support they would like to access to enable them to be more independent. To do this, we need commissioning arrangements that allow for versatility.

Alliance contracts are deliberately flexible, leaving space for people to innovate, respond to changing needs and wants, and for personalised support and services for individuals. These benefit people directly and also give staff permission and confidence to influence what assistance is available. The Future Pathways Alliance in Scotland is a great example here. It has devolved financial decision making to those working with the people it has been set up to support, which has resulted in highly personalised and individualised commissioning (see Case Study 3).

Simple or complex

A similar issue to the knowns and unknowns concerns the level of complexity of the system. The number of organisations involved can be a proxy for this. I realise that you can have complexity even with one or two organisations, but, in the main, the more organisations involved in a system, the more complex it is likely to be.

In other sectors, there are alliances with just one owner (commissioner) and one delivery organisation (provider). Here it is about managing risks collaboratively and working closely together. There is less emphasis on co-ordination across a system.

In public services, apart from small, discrete areas of activity, there are almost always multiple interfaces, relationships and parties – in other words, complex systems. Moving to an alliance means you can refocus attention on to the experience for those using the support and services, not the individual organisations and their specific activity.

As stated earlier, we recommend that an alliance has no more than eight members because the principle of unanimous decision making gets more difficult in practice with higher numbers. This may mean that there are some organisations that form the alliance and others that sit outside. This happens in several of our alliances where there is a group of organisations that are collectively responsible for planning, co-ordination and some of the delivery while working with others as subcontractors or network partners for other services.

The commissioners' role

Commissioners who choose an alliance way of working recognise the value of collaboration and their role in enabling a collaborative environment. If commissioners prefer to allocate risk and manage that through a single or lead provider, then alliance contracting is not for them. I sometimes have someone ask about the individual or organisation to blame (or 'one butt to kick') when things go wrong, which tells me they are not yet ready for an alliance.

To create an alliance way of working, commissioners have to trust and be able to demonstrate that they trust. They must let go of describing detailed service specifications and long lists of performance metrics, or of raising dispute notices as soon as something slips. They need to be system leaders, role modelling a mature approach to the complex interactions and interdependencies that are all around.

A dominant player

In some systems there is a dominant player in terms of size and/or influence, so any collaboration you are planning will need to include them. If the people in that organisation are indicating reluctance to join a risk-sharing collaboration, then you need to think twice. Is it just because they want to hold on to their dominant position and don't want to move to equality in decision making? Is it because the organisation is misaligned, and that success for the alliance will mean they lose out in some way?

We have some alliances with large and influential organisations who have readily taken on the collaborative way of working. It can take time and a lot of reassurance to work through the issues initially, but it is definitely worth it.

On the other hand, in one case we all worked for 18 months on a very promising development, and then one major influential partner engineered that the project rejected alliancing. Their reluctance to move to equal representation and their existing dominance meant that any initial enthusiasm fell away as the reality of what an alliance would entail became evident.

If you think there may be a dominant organisation, take time to understand its situation and why it might be hesitant. You can then consider alternative scopes and remits of your alliance or a different pace in order to get them on board. Or you could develop an alliance in such a way that it operates alongside a major player, in the first instance at least. Once the alliance is established, confidence may grow and their concerns may lessen, as happened in the Future Pathways Alliance in Scotland. This was launched before approval was granted for the NHS partner to be included in the alliance contract, but the approvals needed more time than the start-up phase allowed. The NHS representatives contributed from the start and were part of the Alliance Leadership Team throughout. After some months the contract could be signed, with amendments after one year.

To recap, below are some points about alliances in general, when to choose and when not to choose them – along with some reasons for not choosing an alliance. Put more positively, an alliance is very suitable where there is:

* opportunity and potential for change and innovation over time
* a desire for flexibility in delivery at an individual level
* a complex system with multiple interfaces, relationships and parties
* commitment from the commissioner to leading and contributing to a cultural shift towards collaboration
* a likely group of organisations that are keen to collaborate and commit to sharing risk and responsibility.

Co-commissioning

Co-commissioning an alliance represents a willingness to work together and pool funds so they can be used flexibly. The way in which commissioners commit to working together and finding ways around silo working is a powerful endorsement of collaboration and a precursor to further innovation and co-operation.

Alliances are a great way to move out of silos and arrange support and services around people and communities. To do this well, an alliance needs genuinely pooled funding so it can flex and adapt to best support people on the ground. Removing silos starts with commissioners. Where there are strong relationships between individuals and organisations, moving to co-commissioning and pooling of funds is easier. It is very powerful when commissioners who hold different pots of money demonstrate their commitment to collaboration by becoming co-commissioners and enabling the pooling of the funding they hold on behalf of the people they serve.

Restrictions around funding

The way funding flows from central and local government often means that different people or organisations are charged with arranging different parts of a system. Seen in isolation, each pot may be used well for the purpose intended and show good value for money. Yet the person trying to access support and services may meet barriers to entry because they don't fit the criteria or they get moved from one service to another as one can only carry out a specific activity within the strictures of the allocated funding.

Alliances can make a big difference, but only if the commissioners who control different pots are willing to work together to pool funding and delegate decisions to the alliance. This requires both the will to do so and determination to work through any technical issues.

Public funds, quite rightly, have strict rules and regulations regarding their use. In order to pool funding, there is likely to be a need for a legal agreement. In the Lambeth examples, the pooled fund between a local authority and an NHS body in England was enabled by an agreement made under Section 75 of National Health Services Act 2006.

Ideally, once funds are pooled the alliance should be able to use them for any activity that helps achieve the outcomes. For example, it would be problematic if it could only use the proportion that came from health on designated clinical services as this would stifle innovation and collaboration.

There may also be reporting and accountability lines that make it hard to put into place a genuinely pooled funding allocation. However it should be pursued as far as possible. Early identification of this issue and tackling it head on from the outset will help.

Statutory teams

Several of our alliances work successfully alongside other teams. It sometimes feels as though they would have even more impact if other linked services, often statutory ones, were included. However, it is complicated to untangle finance and governance within a large statutory organisation in order for a team or department to move to working semi-autonomously as part of an alliance. Working through any issues would cause delays; so, as a pragmatic approach, alliances have gone ahead regardless.

Examples of this include the Lambeth Living Well Network Alliance, which includes the council's mental health social work teams, and the Plymouth Alliance, which works closely with council-based teams for homelessness, but these teams are not in the Alliance itself. As long as there is the will, close working between those in an alliance and those outside it is perfectly possible.

Different footprints

If the commissioners all come from the same local authority, there will be no boundary or footprint issues. However, if the local authority is working with health, police and justice or other commissioners, then they are likely to have different jurisdictions. It is usually possible to work through this, although identifying the funding allocation from the larger footprint commissioner can be problematic. We therefore advocate taking a practical approach, using 'good enough' criteria rather than exact science.

The Lambeth Alliances were co-commissioned by Lambeth Council and what was then Lambeth Clinical Commissioning Group (CCG). They both have the borough of Lambeth as their remit, but one is focused on residents in general and the other on those registered with a local GP practice. This is a minor difference, and we were able to describe the scope of this alliance thus: 'The target population includes all those people registered with a Lambeth GP and those ordinarily resident in the borough.'

A more significant difference is present in an alliance under development involving several co-commissioners and multiple layers: one commissioner operates at a local borough level, another covers three boroughs and a third is regional. This will require the larger footprint organisations to identify funding at the borough level and ensure they have the necessary approvals and delegations in place to allow the funding to be pooled – difficult but not impossible.

The lead commissioner

In an alliance everyone is equal, so we usually try to avoid using the word 'lead'. However, on a practical level, one or more members might take the lead on some aspect of the activity. If there is more than one commissioner, there are a couple of reasons why it may be helpful to consider one of them as the 'lead'.

First, there are statutory regulations around public sector commissioning, and these may differ, for example, between local authorities and the NHS. This was a consideration when we set up the Lambeth Alliances. For various reasons, the NHS commissioner, Lambeth CCG as it was then, took a lead. This meant we had to follow the statutory requirement to use NHS standard contracts. Had we been able to nominate Lambeth Council as the lead commissioner, we would not have needed to do this.

In other places, where possible, we have recommended the local authority as a lead commissioner as they usually have more discretion regarding how they contract, although there are other possible impacts and restrictions that need consideration.

The second reason to have a 'lead' commissioner is a pragmatic one. Even where there are only two commissioners, we have tended to have one take the lead for both reporting and accountability of the alliance, and for representation on the Alliance Leadership Team. This is good role modelling for trust and collaboration as well as being of practical benefit.

Contract options appraisal

Even when it looks highly likely that an alliance approach will be a good one, we advocate a rigorous contract options appraisal. This will stand you in good stead for the future, especially if your choice of an alliance is questioned or challenged, as you will be able to say with confidence that you looked at all the options carefully and that the alliance approach scored highest.

A contract options appraisal process is strengthened when it involves a range of people and perspectives. This will also help in disseminating information about your plans, build relationships and trust and create a basis for risk management. Of course, it may also result in the option for an alliance being rejected, but it is best to know that now before you expend further time and energy.

The process we describe here is our 'gold standard' for an options appraisal. You can, as many people do, just write a paragraph or section in a business case document yourself. Sometimes this is necessary as there is no time for anything more. However, this can be a missed opportunity, and it may turn out that you will spend any time saved at a later date because you lack a robust and authentic options appraisal.

Note that we only talk about the contract options at this stage. You may also want to consider different procurement routes – a separate, albeit often linked, issue that we will come to later.

Overview

The overall idea is to involve as many perspectives as you can to help you agree the criteria and score your options. Fig 1.1 sets out the steps in the process.

You will need everyone to have a reasonable understanding of the different options so they can make informed comments during the scoring. I recommend a half-day session at the very least. The process needs some pre-work, the half-day session and then writing up.

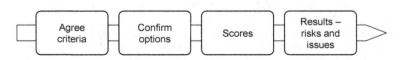

Figure 1.1 Options appraisal process

Pre-work

Set a date and invite people to the group session

Ideally, you should have a range of perspectives at the session to help you score the options – such as from commissioning, legal, finance and procurement colleagues, providers, people with lived experiences and partner organisations.

It can also be useful to invite those who may have some reservations about alliancing. You don't want to only have cheerleaders. Involving people early is beneficial, and the session will be a good opportunity to hear their views and concerns. Set the date well in advance to ensure key people can attend.

Criteria

The options appraisal exercise is designed to answer the question 'Which option will best help us achieve our strategic objectives?' Therefore you need to pull together a list of already stated objectives, for instance from a recent council strategy or your organisation's annual or three-year plan. You may need to merge sets from two or more organisations if you are co-commissioning. Either way, try to create a short list (5–8 items) of strategic objectives.

Next you may want to add some key imperatives, which might be around driving collaboration, making efficiencies or finding alternative income streams. Or there may be practical considerations, such as commissioner capacity and capability. Again, keep these to the essentials only, and don't have too many.

Options

There will be a number of contract options for consideration – typically for separate individual services, lead contractor and alliance. You may also want to add partnerships, consortia or any other approach you have been considering as a collaboration model.

The group session will include people who are not familiar with the language of contracts, so it helps to prepare and distribute a fact sheet in advance and dedicate some time at the beginning of the session to talk through the options. It can be hard to find a balance between technical (jargon) and everyday language, so it is best to err on the side of the latter.

The group session

By way of example, I use the following structure:

1. introductions and scene-setting
2. confirm the criteria

3. confirm the options
4. undertake scoring
5. results – and risks and issues.

Intro and scene-setting

The session is a good opportunity to bring everyone up to speed with progress and ideas. You should also set the tone for your alliance development by being welcoming, inclusive, curious, and so on. Take time to introduce people, using an ice-breaker if appropriate. I like to use one that grounds people in the place, for instance by asking everyone to say what their first memory of the town, city or borough is. That brings in a good mix of people – long-term residents, more recent incomers and others who live elsewhere but work in the location. Their individual stories will then be a mix of funny and poignant with lots of human interest, which helps show that the session is about people even when talking about contracts.

We then move on to the task in hand. Someone can go through progress to date and any other context-setting, leaving time for questions and clarification.

Criteria

Next you can check everyone is happy with the criteria. Talk through the drafts you have put together, explaining the reasoning and what they mean. Leave time for people to challenge them or make other suggestions, and then put these to the room for debate and decision. You want people to feel they have had an input and not feel rushed. End this section by checking everyone is happy with the final list you have collectively created.

Contract options

Do the same checking with the room with the contract options. Again you may need to go through the ones you have, explaining what they mean and how they differ from each other. Before moving on, you can confirm that everyone is ready.

Scoring

Now it is time for the scoring, which I find works best in the following sequence:

1. Everyone scores individually.
2. People compare their scores in groups.
3. All the scores are collated – either individually or by groups.

This last point depends on the numbers in the room: if there are up to, say, 15 people, you can do it individually, but with any more than this it can be quite time-consuming. We once had nearly 30 people, so arranged them into groups to come up with a shared score and then collated the group scores. The scoring system we use is relatively simple:

High = high chance of meeting the criteria
Medium = medium chance of meeting the criteria
Low = low chance of meeting the criteria.

Commonly, people also go for a mix (e.g. H/M or M/L), so you end up with five possible marks.

Results

I try to have a wall chart or master version that you can project so that everyone can see the results as they come in – thus making it a very transparent and open process. As an alliance facilitator, it can be a bit disconcerting if an alliance is not scoring highly, but this hasn't happened to me yet.

If there are a wide range of views on any specific criteria, I ask people to elaborate as it is always fascinating to see how individuals view things quite differently. Such conversations are illuminating and good for everyone to hear. For example, people will often say 'I gave it a High but what if . . .?', and then go on to describe a specific situation that may arise. This is rich information and needs to be captured. In particular, the comments will reveal a lot about the potential risks and issues. If you using groups, ask someone in each group to note the main points from their discussion and have someone do the same for the whole group discussion as you finalise the results. These notes and comments will provide the basis for a comprehensive risk and issues log.

Once all the scores are collated, you can calculate which option had the highest overall score.

Writing up

After the event, as well as thanking people for their time, expertise and views, you can send them a summary of the results and discussions. The summary will have many future uses as the record of the event and the results.

This is a thorough and inclusive process for developing your highest scoring contract option, after which you will be able to refer to it should anyone question or challenge the decision to use an alliance approach. The process also signals your inclusive, collaborative way of working, and helps produce a risk and issue log from different perspectives.

Commissioner readiness

Before you even begin to consider whether an alliance is suitable for the commissioning you are about to undertake, it is important to be realistic about whether you, your team and your organisation are ready to work in a different way. Without question, the role of the commissioner(s) and their readiness to embrace a new way of working are among the most critical factors for setting up a successful alliance.

An alliance is more than a way of working; it is a way of being and a way of thinking. And that needs to extend – not just to the person who is leading the change but also to those around them, especially senior people in executive, finance and legal roles. For example, I have seen every combination – from a committed Commissioner Manager with senior support and helpful finance, legal and procurement colleagues through to a lone Commissioning Manager who had to battle every step of the way. I have seen Commissioning Managers who were told to use an alliance approach but who were clearly not ready to 'let go'. Or there may be a change in Commissioning Manager after the alliance has been set up and the incoming one is not as aware of the new role and what it entails.

An honest appraisal of your own situation and your own organisational readiness will help you to target your efforts. We always recommend starting as early as possible in bringing your colleagues alongside. Don't wait until you are quite far down the road before talking with legal, procurement and finance colleagues as their questions and challenges will be helpful in anticipating the common concerns that arise around alliances.

Commissioner capabilities

An alliance requires a different approach from the commissioner. In essence, you are inviting others to join you in helping you perform your statutory functions or duties. Instead of saying 'You do this bit' and 'You do that bit', you are saying 'Let's do this together.'

This is not just about getting everyone else to work together; it is also about how you work together with everyone else. The commissioners will no longer be the final decision makers on operational and other issues. You move from being a hierarchical leader to a collaborative one. Your role modelling of openness, curiosity, a focus on values and on what people have said matters to them is critical. Are you ready for such change?

Commissioner roles

The roles and accountability needed for an alliance are covered in more detail later, but it is important to understand the two linked but distinct roles of commissioners: as 'owners' and as 'participants'.

Commissioners as owners

The 'owner' role is similar to the usual role in commissioning: you set the mandate, the outcomes and the funding envelope for the alliance; and once it is up and running, there is a hands-off approach. There will be regular reports about progress against the outcomes, including financial ones, but no need for contract monitoring meetings going through pages of data and quibbling over details. This is because the Alliance Leadership Team will be looking at performance and finance information at all their meetings. They will then use that information to plan ahead, set strategy and ensure the right capabilities and capacity are in place; and, should any difficulties arise, the Alliance Leadership Team will manage and address them.

The 'Commissioner as Owner' role is usually embodied by a senior person – the Chief Executive Officer (CEO), Director of Finance or Director of Commissioning. If there is more than one commissioning organisation, there will be named people in each; or, as in some of our alliances, the role is embodied by a joint committee.

Commissioners as alliance participants

It is this second role that represents the biggest change for commissioners– being an active member of an alliance. This is about becoming an equal with provider member representatives and working collaboratively with them to share responsibility for leading and governing the alliance.

One or more commissioner representatives are part of the Alliance Leadership Team. These must be different people to those functioning as Commissioner as Owner because it is impossible to be an equal member one moment and an owner the next.

The Alliance Leadership Team meetings replace contract monitoring meetings. Instead of monitoring against terms of a contract, everyone is relentlessly focused on best performance against the outcomes and their contribution to achieving them.

In my experience, this shared decision making takes a while to settle into the new way of working. Often in a procurement process the commissioner has been examiner and judge, with the providers doing what they have been told to do and waiting to hear whether they have 'passed'. Going from this dynamic to one where all are equal around the table will take time. The commissioner representatives need to demonstrate the change in how they behave and interact with the group.

Collaborative leadership

The commissioner representatives on the Alliance Leadership Team need to be collaborative leaders first and foremost. I find that commissioners who

Table 1.1 Commissioner roles in traditional and alliance contracts

Traditional	Alliance
Parent/child relationship	Adult-adult relationship
Co-ordinator between parties	As owner, set the mandate, specify
Fixer of interface issues and interparty disputes	outcomes and reporting against these
Multiple contract monitor	As alliance member, continuing role alongside other members
	Focus on system and role model leadership
= hierarchical/transactional leader	One leadership forum replaces contract monitoring
	= collaborative leader

have led alliance developments tend to be innately collaborative, which is why they choose alliances in the first place. The Alliance Leadership Team and the role of the commissioner representatives on it embody the change in relationship between commissioners and providers.

The wider commissioning organisation

Moving to an alliance way of working means changes for others in commissioning organisations. Awareness of and preparation for the changes for individuals and teams will help the alliance from the outset. Investment in people through time and resources will put the commissioning organisation in a strong position as a role model and instigator of the new way of working in the future.

If possible it is helpful to have a generally available leadership and development programme for people in all roles – finance, legal, procurement, performance as well as commissioning ones. Through this, preparation for new relationships and capabilities will be widespread. Usually, alliancing is adopted alongside a greater commitment to working with communities and citizens, so there is plenty of scope for creating an exciting and immersive cultural change programme.

Of course, the alliance may only be one small initiative and all other activity remains the same, meaning that people will be in 'old'-style mode for some parts of their work and alliance mode for others. I have heard people say this is a reason not to adopt alliancing. My response is informed by spending time with people in other sectors. There, organisations and businesses that are much smaller than many public sector ones, or even the larger charities, are very adept at simultaneously running traditional service contracts alongside various types of partnerships and alliances.

Commissioner capacity

Development of an alliance takes time and energy, and will need a few people to be closely involved for many months. Some thoughts about your capacity and that of your team will help keep things moving. Any change requires commitment and resilience; and, although the larger the change, the more you would think these are needed, we find that even small-scale alliances can take a lot of time and energy to set up.

Having worked with lots of different people and teams leading alliance developments, I can safely say that there is no perfect model. In the reality of the UK public sector at the time of writing this book, there is unlikely to be the luxury of overcapacity.

Project lead/Commissioning Manager

The pivotal person in every alliance I have been involved in has been a committed and visionary Commissioning Manager: someone who really wants to put people front and centre; someone who can manage the intricacies and politics of getting a change programme up and running in a pressurised environment; someone who understands the content area and all the surrounding stakeholder dynamics.

I have every respect for anyone in this role as they are often juggling a wider portfolio and the alliance is only one of their responsibilities. My advice is to look after yourself and ensure you have support, be that from senior colleagues, peers or a team around you. There will be tough days as well as good days. As mentioned, creating an alliance is a long and often difficult process. It is a big change programme and needs to be resourced as such. No one person can do this alone.

Project teams

The following are two fictional examples, although based on real-life cases.

TEAM A

From the time an alliance approach was first considered, the Commissioning Manager set up a fortnightly project meeting. This brought together people from different commissioning teams in two commissioning organisations, along with procurement, finance and legal colleagues, and the lead Commissioning Manager and his administration support. At times, others were invited and special meetings held. The team met regularly for over 18 months to develop and implement the Alliance Strategy, project plans and procurement process.

TEAM B

The Commissioning Manager leading the development appointed a part-time project manager. The two of them successfully obtained approval for their Alliance Strategy, and developed the prospectus and procurement process with the help of procurement colleagues. They led the whole development over 18 months.

You will have your own reflections about these examples, and may recognise where you and your team sit in relation to them. Circumstances may dictate how close you will be to Example A or Example B. Both have advantages and disadvantages.

A large project team meeting regularly allows everyone to remain up to speed with all the issues. You avoid the situation of having to brief, for example, the legal advisers, about the overall plan in order to discuss a particular query. Everyone understands the whole. However, this demands a lot of everyone's time, even if travel time is reduced now we are used to virtual meetings in the aftermath of Covid-19. Meetings can be repetitive, especially if not much progress has been made between sessions.

A small project team can be very effective, flexible and able to keep people informed through one-to-one discussions rather than group meetings. This does, however, put a lot of pressure on the individuals. As a minimum I would advise that a dedicated full-time project manager is needed.

Specialist advisers

At different times you will need legal, procurement, finance and communications input. Again, it will be very specific to your context as to whether people join a regular meeting with you or are called on as needed.

Commissioner approval

I often say that getting commissioners' sign-off to proceed is the most time-consuming part of getting ready for an alliance. Large organisations with responsibilities for commissioning public services will have several layers of committees and meetings that all need to approve a major change.

Alliancing is a new approach, so people rightly want to scrutinise it in detail. There are always numerous valid questions when you are moving away from the conventions of usual services contracts. You often need the formal approval of different groups and committees, not just the most senior one, such as the Cabinet.

A good strategy and business case

The first task here is to collate all developments and analysis to date into a single document. Each organisation has its own preferred style and format: some like detailed business cases, while others want a more narrative approach. At the very least, you should anticipate the questions that are likely to arise and have a coherent story to tell. Table 1.2 outlines some examples of the content we used recently.

Table 1.2 Example outline for alliance business case

1. Long-term goals (the what)
   - draw on the goals in recent organisational strategies and plans, and how an integrated approach with statutory agencies, delivery organisations and communities working together will help achieve these
   - describe a co-produced set of outcomes as a mechanism to show progress and encourage learning and continuous improvement
2. Benefits (the why)
For people:
   - minimises 'handovers' and the need for eligibility criteria
   - easy to navigate and get help and advice when needed
   - links support and services with prevention
   - creates more capability to move people on
For delivery organisations, including statutory ones:
   - longer contracts to allow planning and investment
   - outcome-based contract, so trusted to develop support and services that work and are right for people
   - flexibility to change support and services over time as demographics, numbers, needs or wants change
   - working alongside organisations with same common goals and similar values
   - part of a system, able to influence and contribute to how the system develops
For commissioners:
   - pooling funds means there is potential for more value for money
   - less duplication and lower overheads (e.g. in letting contracts separately)
   - mandate for alliance is set by commissioners; it exists to deliver the outcomes they set on behalf of the public they serve
   - drives collaborative working focused on people not individual organisations
3. The proposed alliance (the what)
   - what is an alliance? – explain the use of alliance contracting to drive collaboration and innovation, and to foster risk- and responsibility-sharing between all parties
   - contract strategy with options appraisal
   - this alliance – scope and out of scope, purpose and key responsibilities, procurement route, funding allocation, contract length
   - procurement strategy
4. Risks and issues (the but)
   - current services are good, so risk of destabilising what is good
   - multiple commissioners with different footprints and accountabilities
   - complexity of unpicking the current financial, legal and governance arrangements
   - local organisations at different stages of readiness
   - interdependencies with wider services, so risk of only focusing on alliance scope
5. Plan (the how)
   - mindful of the long-term goal and benefits; but, in light of risks and issues, have overall 'roadmap' with indicative time frames with built-in flexibility
   - key dependencies and milestones
   - likely dates and/or sequence

A write-up of the case for change and what you are proposing will help clarify your own thinking as well as inform others.

As well as a formal document, you may want to consider having a short leaflet or description of what you are planning. We created one for the second Lambeth Alliance, explaining the journey so far, the reasons to keep innovating and the plans for the future. It was useful in many situations, including with local people and partner organisations.

Start early

Once again, we advise involving your colleagues and senior people as soon as possible, whether in one-to-one conversations, information sessions or project updates. Their questions, concerns and suggestions about technical aspects will really help work through the issues early and make life easier later on.

It goes without saying that support from senior people is vital. I've seen the benefits of having chief executives and councillors as champions. It helps with getting the whole organisation behind you. As alliances are all about collaboration and putting people front and centre, it is usually something that resonates with people and they are happy to endorse. Similarly, try to use every opportunity to talk with people in your community, partner organisations and the provider market about your plans. Hopefully, they will reinforce the enthusiasm to move to a different way of working, which will help with internal approvals.

Of course, there may be some who do not want to go in this direction. However it is better to know that early on, finding what is behind their concerns and working with them and those they seek to influence before you are further along.

Expect setbacks

Hopefully, there will be no setbacks, but don't be surprised if there are. This is a new approach and, although people can understand it makes sense, it threatens the status quo – and that is often enough to prompt some challenges.

Plan the timeline

Make sure you know the dates of the key meetings where approval for the strategy and plans is required. Some of these may have a deadline of 2–3 weeks in advance for paper submissions, and even longer for agenda requests. If more than one commissioner is involved, you will need to consider each of them.

For example, on one occasion we used a large, multicoloured A3 chart just for the timeline for approvals by two commissioning organisations. It covered several months, and any date or milestone that was missed had a big knock-on effect on all the others. My advice therefore is to lay everything out well in advance and keep checking you are on track.

Repeat frequently

There is often a time lag between all the approvals and the launch of the alliance. After all the activity involved when starting the alliance development, it is easy to forget that people will have moved on to thinking about other things, or they may have left their role and been replaced by new people.

We recently had an example where colleagues in the commissioning organisation who were not close to the alliance had slipped back into, let's say, 'old thinking'. This was causing some difficulties for the alliance in being able to move forward confidently with their delegated authority. Refreshers about what alliances entail and how they work were therefore needed.

You will want continued approval, not just one-off permission to get started. Therefore, schedule in updates on the alliance and how it is going, as well as reminders about the alliance way of working.

Summary

Setting up an alliance can feel overwhelming. There are many questions and much to think about. Taking a systematic approach will help address all the issues and create a solid foundation on which to proceed.

You will want your colleagues to be alongside you, so involve them early and consider how you all can move from your current way of working to new collaborative roles. Start early and repeat frequently. A clear Alliance Strategy, informed by different perspectives and addressing the challenges and risks, will be an important document with many uses. At this early stage, you can describe what you expect to achieve and the path you plan to take to get there.

In the next chapter we will add a lot more detail to your vision and plans.

References

Australia National Audit Office. (2001). *Contract management: Best practice guide.* Commonwealth of Australia. https://catalogue.nla.gov.au/catalog/1113578.

Ross, J. (2009). *Alliance contracting in Australia: A brief introduction.* IQPC alliance masterclass. Unpublished, used with permission.

Case study 2

Stockport – The Prevention Alliance (2015–present)

The Prevention Alliance (TPA) delivers support to enable people in Stockport to improve their confidence, independence, health and well-being. It has strong local connections, and works in partnership with local organisations to ensure people can access a diverse range of support options.

The Prevention Alliance was commissioned by the Stockport Metropolitan Borough Council with six voluntary and community organisations. The new service went live on 1 July 2015 with an annual budget of £1.5 million. The contract was initially for three years with an option for a one-year extension, but TPA was still operating in 2024.

Creating the Alliance

In 2014/15, faced with an impending reduction to the budget and with a desire to move to a more generic preventative approach led by need rather than 'specific' support according to groups (e.g. carers, people with disabilities, older people), Stockport Council was aware that a completely new approach was needed to commissioning and service provision. Prior to this there were around 60 separate contracts and grants with charities, not-for-profit and independent organisations, some of which were coming to the end of their term. After undertaking an options appraisal, the council decided an alliance contract would best deliver on its strategic objectives.

The council had experience with alliance contracting through the Stockport Enablement and Recovery Alliance, set up in April 2013. This was a small, short-term alliance that acted as a test for the alliance way of working. The council chose the group of organisations through open-market procurement and launched TPA, whose members bring a wide range of expertise, including housing, older people and relationship support.

Progress of the Alliance

TPA set up the Stockport Support Hub – a single point of access for anyone in the borough (Greater Manchester) seeking support and advice for themselves or others. Access is by phone or online, and requests can come from local people or professionals. The requests are triaged and responded to with signposting or offers of support. The Alliance also provides short-term support with key workers for up to six months. Longer-term support was initially available, but the remit changed over time. It works closely with partners in supported housing, carer support and domestic abuse services as well as local initiatives such as DigiKnow, which promotes online access for all.

In its first couple of years there were some changes to member organisations: one changed focus and moved away from delivery (leaving the Alliance by mutual consent): and another became part of a bigger group but remained a member of the Alliance. Around this time, relationships with Stockport Council started to change. When the commissioner who had set up the Alliance left, those who followed were less familiar with an alliance way of working, so there were times when commissioner representatives defaulted to traditional behaviours. Over time, attendance by council representatives waned and the Alliance Leadership Team became provider only. TPA continues to provide the council with detailed quarterly reports.

This evolution from alliance contract to business-to-business alliance was complete when activities were recommissioned in 2022. The council had moved away from specifically wanting an alliance, and asked for bids for different elements of the prevention work. TPA members wanted to continue to work together and bid collectively. They won the bid for a large part of their previous remit, thus continuing as The Prevention Alliance.

The Prevention Alliance as a brand and first port of call for anyone in the borough remains strong. Their role includes some specialisms, such as support for the deaf community. Their annual budget fell over the years due to the ongoing local fiscal environment and with the recent refocus, and now stands at just under £1 million.

There remains a deep sense of collaboration between TPA members. Despite changes in personnel, several people have been part of the Alliance since the beginning. They talk about the challenges (that it is not always easy) and how the Alliance Principles allow them to work through any difficulties, especially 'best for Alliance'. They say they are so steeped in that way of working that it comes naturally. It is often only when they are in other groupings that they realise others do not have that same sense of collaboration. Relationships are key and at the core of all they do. These personnel worked hard at creating a unified culture, and commented that this takes longer than you think. A workforce survey showed that all responders felt proud to work for TPA, so the effort has paid off well.

Overall, there is recognition that some things are harder than others; for instance, variations in terms and conditions will always be present and controversial. However, there is unanimous agreement that the benefits of working in an alliance outweigh the downsides.

What changed for people

For individuals who contact the Alliance, the impact on their well-being is tracked and it is clear the support is helpful and, for some, life-changing. Local teams and professionals praise the ease of referrals to Stockport Support Hub.

Longer time or community-wide impacts are less visible despite being part of the outcomes stipulated at the outset. Evidence of short-term impacts was initially prioritised by the council and other evaluations dropped. It is clear though that TPA is now seen as the lead for prevention across the borough, and highly valued. One of the drivers for creating the Alliance was the lack of co-ordinated support. However, this changed as Stockport Support Hub developed into the single point of access and co-ordination.

For more information see: https://www.stockporttpa.co.uk/.

2 Alliance mandate

For an alliance to be successful, everyone involved needs to be clear about what it has been set up to achieve and for whom. How the alliance proceeds may change over time, but its core purpose and overall objectives will be stipulated from the outset. Getting these right is critical for all alliances. It can be an instructive and collective endeavour to take initial thoughts and ideas and hone them into to a coherent narrative about what an alliance is about and what it is expected to achieve. This is the 'Alliance Mandate'.

In this chapter we will go through the core purpose, objectives and other essential building blocks for an alliance – the foundations on which everything else stands. At the end of the chapter you will have the content for your Alliance Mandate. This can then be used for procurement documents and in discussions with potential members of your alliance or other dialogues you need to have.

Introduction to Alliance Mandate

When people are thinking about creating an alliance they might start at any number of places. There might already be a group of organisations that are keen to work together – or not. They might have a clear idea of specifically what the alliance will do, or they may only be at an initial idea stage. They might have been working with people and organisations to develop ideas about how support and services can improve and be arranged in the future. Or this may be something that is yet to happen.

There are often many questions and issues buzzing around: What about this, what about that, have you thought of x, what shall we do about y? To make sense of these different starting points and the many unknowns, I find it helpful to break things down to bite-sized chunks and work through. Typically, I would do this with people over a series of discussions and meetings that take place over weeks and even months. Over time, these discussions feed into the Alliance Mandate.

DOI: 10.4324/9781003511809-2

In essence, the Alliance Mandate is the instruction given to the alliance by the owner – or, using the term we are familiar with from the previous chapter, the 'Commissioner as Owner'. In the public sector, alliances are usually set up by a local authority, health commissioner or government department.

The Commissioner as Owner needs to describe what and for whom the alliance is being set up: What will it focus on? What are the outcomes the Commissioner as Owner hopes it will achieve for people? What do people say matters to them? Other considerations include funding allocation, the length of the contract and any service standards that need to be met.

The alliance will only exist to deliver what the Commissioner as Owner asks it to deliver. It is not like a business-to-business collaboration that might also seek other work elsewhere. The alliance is accountable to the Commissioner as Owner throughout its lifetime for delivering the Mandate.

Once the content of the Alliance Mandate is finalised, it can be used as the specification or proposition for any procurement process to select members of the alliance. Therefore it needs to contain enough detail about the proposed alliance for organisations to decide whether they want to bid for membership.

Before we start, let's look at a few terms and general points.

Alliance Charter and Alliance Mandate

These two terms are frequently used in relation to alliances. The term 'Alliance Charter' is used for a short description of an alliance, its purpose, objectives and values. The Alliance Charter forms the first part of the Alliance Agreement, the legal deed, and is also helpful in communications with partner organisations and the public.

In adapting alliance contracting in the UK public sector, we found we needed both an Alliance Charter and something that builds on it, adding information about contract length and funding allocation. To keep them separate, we use the term 'Alliance Mandate'. The different terms and what I mean by them is given in Table 2.1.

Whose alliance is it anyway?

Developing the Alliance Mandate is a role for the Commissioner as Owner. In public sector alliances, the commissioners are acting on behalf of the public they serve. The Alliance Mandate must therefore reflect the views and perspectives of those who the support and services will be for. Co-designing the Alliance Mandate is essential for its legitimacy.

Our alliances usually develop where there is awareness that current services are not meeting the expectations of those they serve. Someone in a commissioning role in a local authority, health commissioner or government department is looking to drive collaboration and innovation in the set

Table 2.1 Alliance Charter and Alliance Mandate

	Alliance Charter	Alliance Mandate
Description	A summary of the purpose, role and principles of the Alliance	The core information about what the Alliance is being set up for and what the Commissioner as Owner expects from it.
Main purpose	For communications once the Alliance is set up	For procurement and reporting
Usual content	Includes: • Vision • Purpose • Objectives • Outcomes • Scope • Principles • Values and behaviours	As for Alliance Charter plus: • Funding allocation • Contract length • Alliance governance • Service standards

of services and support for a community or defined group of people. In their role, they are acting on behalf of those people – for example the residents of a particular place, children and young people with a specific set of circumstances, the citizens of a borough, town or city. The commissioners act as the vehicle for translating the aspirations, wishes and needs of citizens or groups of citizens into sets of support and services for them.

It is imperative therefore that the Alliance Mandate has been informed and shaped by people who have experience of and understand what is required – namely, those who use services and those with relevant lived experiences. It might also include people who work closely with people and understand the issues on the ground.

Starting with their views and input makes the Alliance Mandate authentic, strong and relevant. The more it reflects different people and different perspectives, the better it will be. It will have legitimacy and be able to be referenced even when there are inevitable concerns and difficult times.

Many public sector commissioners are good at working with citizens and service providers to co-design strategies and design new pathways. There are many examples of groups and conversations set up to do this, and people will have given their time and ideas over many meetings over long periods of time. This is excellent and gives a strong platform for going forward.

It is usually possible to turn all the rich information and ideas into content for the Alliance Mandate. However, in some places, this step has not yet taken place. We would advise that new conversations and activities be set up to gain further information and ensure that the Mandate truly reflects the views of those for whom it is being set up.

Now let's turn to the steps to build the content of an Alliance Mandate.

Earlier we used the dictionary definition of an alliance as 'an agreement between two or more individuals or entities stating that the involved parties will act in a certain way in order to achieve a common goal'. This provides us with a structure (building blocks) to work through as we develop the Alliance Mandate.

The common goal

Vision

It is important to have an overarching statement of your vision – a single phrase or sentence that encapsulates the ideal or dream future. That is what a vision should be.

It is surprisingly difficult to write a vision. A statement about ending poverty or homelessness or 'Everyone lives a full and healthy life' will have some people saying that it is too 'highbrow', it is 'motherhood' and 'apple pie'. Others will say it is unachievable and so there is no point stating it.

Yet it is essential to draw people together, and I would strongly recommend having a vision statement. You might have heard about a 'North Star' or 'Big Hairy (Audacious) Goals' (BHAGs) or other such terms. The vision is the same idea – a statement of that end point you are all working towards.

If you can get the vision statement right, you will end up using it in material aimed at many different audiences, so it is worth honing it at the beginning. We sometimes do this as a group exercise, asking everyone to write down their version, and then comparing notes at tables or in pairs and then

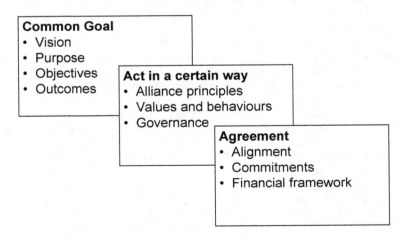

Figure 2.1 The building blocks for an alliance

as a whole group. It usually ends with people taking quite strong positions. Visions matter.

Of course, you can use the vision you already have. Most public sector organisations will already have one. Local authorities will have three- or five-year strategies created with citizens and partners. These strategies will usually have started by setting out a vision. If this is the case, you can use what is already there. You may have to tweak it for the groups or people you are creating your alliance for, but usually that is not needed. For instance, if the strategy for young people says something like 'All children can fulfil their potential', then, even if your alliance is for individuals with autism or long-term health conditions, for instance, the overarching vision still holds.

MY RULES FOR VISION

Here are my rules for writing a vision statement, followed by a few examples:

- It must be written from the perspective of people, not services.
- It can only be one sentence if possible, otherwise two at most.
- It must be in plain English – no jargon.

Example 1: In Lambeth, long before they started considering an alliance contract approach, they had set up the Lambeth Living Well Collaborative. Its core is a group of people who meet once a month in a local café for breakfast. The group includes people with experience of mental health issues, either personally or through someone close to them, frontline workers, local charities, the NHS mental health trust, health commissioners and the local authority. These meetings are a time for discussions and ideas and, from the outset, several new initiatives developed, most of them peer-led or involving people with lived experience of mental health distress.

In the early days (2010/11), participants developed their shared vision and what became their three big outcomes, running specific events and forums to hear from as many people as possible. The vision and outcomes are very well established, and were the guiding lights when we came to develop alliances in Lambeth. The Lambeth Living Well Collaborative vision reads:

Every citizen, whatever their abilities or disabilities, can flourish, contribute to society and lead the life they want to lead.

It is one sentence, in plain English and only about people. There is no mention of support, services, helping, supporting or any of the words that often sneak back into service speak. Using this for their alliance meant that they had the freedom to think about ways of making this happen that have absolutely nothing to do with services or support. The vision establishes an environment where anything is possible.

Example 2: A similar example comes from an alliance in Glasgow, whose vision could not have been simpler:

> The vision for the Alliance is to end homelessness in Glasgow.

It was clear and powerful, and belonged to the Glasgow Alliance to End Homelessness. Some may say this was too bold given this alliance ended early, but I still support the clarity that the vision gave (see Case Study 7).

Example 3: Here we had some work to do. This is the nearest there was to a vision statement in the background papers for what was to become one of our other alliances:

> This service aims to improve the lives of people facing multiple disad- vantage by supporting the whole person to meet their aspirations, whilst also contributing towards national outcome targets in relation to statutory homelessness, children in care and care leavers, drug treatment, reoffend- ing rates, preventing admissions to hospital and urgent care targets.

I am sure you can see the difference. This comes from a good, well-meaning place but, after a quick nod to people's aspirations, it becomes about national targets and a list of priorities. It's all about the service and statutory require- ments. What does it really say about people?

We worked to rewrite the statement, with the final version being:

> Our vision is to improve the lives of people facing multiple disadvantage, supporting the whole person to meet their aspirations and to participate in and contribute to all aspects of life.

Although this remains more 'doing to' than ideal, it is an improvement on the first version.

Purpose

The second essential aspect of the alliance building block is a clear statement of purpose – the reason the alliance is needed to achieve the vision. This might seem obvious to you, but it won't always be to everyone else.

If you speak to people in an area affected by the issue(s) the alliance is con- cerned with and tell them the vision, a common response is 'Why aren't you doing that anyway?' People will ask why it needs an alliance to do this; why aren't all the people and organisations working in this field (homelessness, mental health, young people's services) trying to end homelessness, helping everyone fulfil their lives, reach their potential or whatever the vision says?

The answer is that they are all probably trying to achieve the vision, but the way services and support are arranged and financed is making it difficult. It might also be that the way some of them are working with people is too paternalistic; or it might be that more money is going on specialist or crisis services and not enough on prevention and early intervention.

You are setting up your alliance to overcome some or all of these difficulties. This is an opportunity to challenge yourselves as to why you need an alliance to do that. What will the alliance be able to do that you cannot do in a different way?

Over time, we have realised that the purpose of an alliance typically includes phraseology such as 'to lead, manage and co-ordinate . . .' or similar, as in the following examples.

Camden Mental Health Resilience Alliance:

The Alliance is being set up to plan, coordinate and manage a range of support and services for those who are concerned about their own or their family or friend's mental wellbeing. With other partners, it will work to build community resilience and reduce stigma and inequalities in mental health.

Future Pathways:

The purpose of our Alliance is to co-ordinate access to and the delivery of resources, integrated care and support so that Survivors can achieve their own goals.

Cardiff and Vale Alliance:

We are establishing an Alliance to plan, provide, co-ordinate, and continuously improve a range of substance misuse services in Cardiff and the Vale of Glamorgan to deliver the outcomes that people want to see.

You will note in these examples that the purpose relates to the additional thing(s) the alliance does besides delivering services, even though delivery or provision is there in all of them too.

Objectives

Having described the overall vision and why the alliance is being created to achieve it, we shall now talk about its objectives – the small number of core aspects the alliance will focus on.

There is a large body of literature on objectives: SMART (specific, measurable, achievable, relevant and time-bound) objectives, objectives vs goals, objectives vs outcomes, objectives vs values. As someone with a medical and educational background, I am fully aware of these discussions, and also that you can get stuck in definition purity and definition dispute.

Alliances in other sectors have a particular set of objectives. These are used to develop performance measures and, in construction for instance, will cover safety, quality, cost, schedule, disruption and legacy.

When I started talking about alliances in health and social care in 2011/12, the concept of outcomes was moving fast up the agenda. The word 'objectives' was seen as referring to process, whereas 'outcomes' were considered better for describing end points. Therefore I started to use 'outcomes' rather than 'objectives', but my approach was always pragmatic. If some outcomes felt process-like, then so be it if that was an important part of what defined success.

For instance, some of our early outcome sets included 'style of delivery' so that you could capture the sense of people being treated with respect, being informed, given choices and so on. Over time, though, I came to realise that you need both objectives and outcomes, differentiated as below:

- Objectives: a few key things that the alliance is expected to focus on from the outset and bring about change from the status quo.
- Outcomes: if we are successful, this is what we will see – for people, for workforces, for communities.

We found that just using outcomes can be so far-reaching that it is hard to remain focused on the here and now.

Most commissioners wanting to set up an alliance have specific things they want it to tackle. They are reluctant to let go of stating these, and solely rely on describing the outcomes that are expected if these are put in place. The time-scales for demonstrating achievement of outcomes can be lengthy and might be affected, positively and negatively, by a range of factors.

Provider members of alliances also find that focusing on a few key elements helps when there is so much going on in the early days of an alliance. For instance, there might be a desire to spend more resources on prevention rather than crisis, with the expectation that this will eventually lead to better outcomes for people and less use of expensive specialist services.

So, the focus for now is to shift resources, and this should be front and centre for all as it might get lost if you only focused on the endpoint. We therefore use objectives as the small number of core things that need to change, as the objectives from the following alliances illustrate.

Example 1 – Lambeth Living Well Network Alliance:

- improve access to support – including easier early access and a rapid crisis response
- integrate and co-ordinate care and support for people and their networks across Lambeth

- reduce the inequalities faced by people experiencing mental health problems
- manage demand and resources effectively
- drive culture change – including leadership and asset-based working.

You can see how these represent things that need to change compared with before the Alliance. You could easily guess that, prior to the Alliance, there were problems regarding access and co-ordination, inequality, demand and culture. This Alliance has to focus on these in all it does.

Example 2 – County Durham's Mental Health and Wellbeing Alliance:

- involve stakeholders, providers and service users in the design and delivery of support and services
- work with communities, supporting their own development and resilience adapting to their assets and needs
- ensure support and services are person-centred and based on people's strengths and aspirations
- create one identity with a co-ordinated pathway so people easily know how to access advice and support for themselves or a family member
- fill gaps in support and services across the county.

Here again you can see the priorities and drivers for the commissioners at Durham County Council at the time. Behind each item will be a good reason it is being flagged up.

USING THE OBJECTIVES

As you write your objectives, remember that a list is only useful if it can be used. At the beginning of an alliance there are a multitude of things to do, including setting up co-ordination, allocating roles, and developing policies and procedures. It is easy to get lost and lose focus, so a set or list of objectives will be of enormous help to remind people – but only if it is easy to remember.

We all know that mission statements, values and principles are often developed with a lot of dialogue and energy, but after a few weeks and months they fade from memory. They certainly will if they are long, wordy lists that can only really be looked at if written down. I am a strong advocate for keeping these core elements to a maximum of five, and ideally four, items.

A positive sign for any alliance is that every member of its leadership and management teams can tell you the vision, purpose and objectives of the alliance if asked – any time, any place and without looking them up. This tells me that they are all very aware and committed to the common goal and have it in mind at every meeting. They will help remind each other when there are difficult conversations and thorny issues to resolve about why they are all here.

Outcomes

As with objectives, outcomes can mean different things to different people. Also, there are some who feel outcomes are not helpful as they drive perverse behaviours and lead to a focus on performance reporting rather than on values and relationships.

I have some sympathy with that argument, but only if you start with the idea that outcomes only reflect one viewpoint and are restricted to things that are easily measured. As Flora Henderson, Alliance Manager for Scotland's Future Pathways Alliance says, 'Relationships are an outcome in themselves.'

In our outcome development work we emphasise two things:

1. that the outcomes simply describe what it would look and feel like if the alliance is successful; and
2. that success needs to be described from a range of perspectives.

In this way, the outcomes become the things that matter to people, in their own words. At this point, it is best not to worry about how the alliance will measure whether the outcome is being met. Some may be very difficult to measure; but, in my view, they should still be there on the page because they matter.

OUTCOMES ON A PAGE

Continuing the theme from the objectives, a short list is better than a long list. Remember that there will be various audiences who are interested in the outcomes, so it is useful to think about how you will present or describe the outcomes to them. We advocate having a high-level version that fits on one page or one slide in a presentation pack. Obviously there will be more detail behind this, but a one-pager is a great tool for making sure you are being succinct as well as useful in talking about the outcomes. The following examples will illustrate.

Example 1 – The Lambeth Alliances

The starting point here was their 'Three Big Outcomes' developed with people well before any alliance was being contemplated:

• to recover and stay well
• to make their own choices
• to participate on an equal footing in daily life.

In the Integrated Personalised Support Alliance (IPSA), we took these outcomes, created some detail and added some more from other perspectives.

Table 2.2 Lambeth IPSA outcomes set

Recovery and staying well	Improved mental health wellbeing People's physical health has been addressed and managed Reduced unplanned use of services
Own choices	People live in a place of their own choosing People use personal budgets
Participation	More people are in employment All take part in meaningful activities
Social value	Improved overall value to the community
Cost	Actual costs equal or less than target costs Cost profile changes in line with plan
Safety	Reduced incidents of safeguarding, self harm and crime

There are a few discussion points here.

1. The set includes cost outcomes: It is common to have a set of performance outcomes with no mention of finances or costs. People talk about performance outcomes with some audiences and financial ones with others. The reports will come from different people and teams who are only focused on their remit. To my mind, this creates a sense that these are not linked, or that success will be counted only by one or the other. Yet, to be successful, you need both – so why not think of them together?

We have always included financial outcomes in everything else. Everyone knows that there is a limited pot of money, so let's be upfront about it. All audiences understand the need to ensure that you keep within the funds available.

In this example, there was also an outcome related to moving funds to prevention activities and away from crisis. Some would argue that this is not an outcome for people. Of course not; but it is a good marker of there being fewer crises needing high-cost interventions. Therefore, including this outcome in the summary list helps focus minds, actions and efforts.

2. Social value: At the time of IPSA's launch, social value had become a priority for Lambeth Council. In general, the use of social value in both outcomes and in bid evaluation has become more common lately and, despite the well-documented problems of measurement, we would expect social value to be included in an outcome set.

3. Safety: Specifying a change to reported incidents is a thorny issue: you don't want to stop people reporting incidents in order to keep numbers down. We debated this at length, and it was agreed to keep this outcome despite this risk. It signals the importance of the issue and, again, will focus minds.

When we came to develop the second iteration, the Living Well Network Alliance, we revisited the original outcomes and refined them. This alliance was for adults experiencing mental distress or most forms of illness, whereas IPSA related only to those with severe and enduring mental health illness. We had to reflect this.

By this point, everyone was familiar with using 'I statements', which we found very helpful. So we changed 'Reduction in the number of people reaching crisis point' to 'I receive early support that helps me avoid reaching crisis point.'

In this way we created a narrative – a way of talking through the steps of our thinking and what we were hearing, which put the set of outcomes into context. On one page you have the full range of perspectives. Most outcomes are about people who use or might use support and services, but there are also the experiences of the workforce and the wider community.

This list was useful at the time of developing the Alliance and thinking about all those perspectives. However, there are 21 subheadings and some of the outcomes are very broad and societal, going beyond the scope and influence of the Alliance. It was therefore recognised that there needed to be some prioritisation.

The Living Well Network Alliance, through consultation and with permission from its Commissioner as Owner, rationalised the list in the first year and created a 12-item version. It later focused further on six and renamed them 'strategic priorities':

- Reduce numbers of people reaching crisis point and give prompt and appropriate support for people in crisis.
- Increase numbers of people able to live independently.
- Increase numbers of people living in stable and appropriate accommodation.
- Improve mental health outcomes for black communities in Lambeth.
- Improve physical health for people with mental health issues.
- Increase numbers of people in education, training, volunteering or employment.

These are now used to demonstrate progress in their annual reports.

This cycle of broad statements, added detail and rationalisation is common as you develop your descriptions of success. On the one hand, there is a lot of effort and it could be short-circuited. On the other, the discussions and inputs from a range of people are instructive and helpful.

Table 2.3 Lambeth Living Well Network Alliance outcomes

Big Three Outcomes	Outcome Area	Outcome	Person Statement
Recovery and staying well	Mental Health	Improvement in people's rating of their own mental health	I feel that my mental health is better
		Increase in the number of people able to live independently	The support that I receive helps me to live independently
	Crisis reduction	Reduction in the number of people reaching crisis point	I receive early support that helps me avoid reaching crisis point
		People in crisis receive prompt and appropriate support	If I experience mental health crisis, I can access support quickly and am treated with dignity and respect
	Physical Health	Reduction in the premature mortality rate for people with mental health issues	I live equally as long as the rest of the population
		Reduction in the physical health issues experienced by people with mental health issues	I am supported to improve my physical health
	Equality	Improvement in the mental health outcomes for people from black communities in Lambeth	I achieve the same outcomes for my mental health regardless of my ethnic or cultural background
Own Choices	Access	Increase in the number of people able to access support in their own homes	I receive support in my own home as much as possible
		Increase in awareness of available support	I know where to go if I feel that I need support
		Increase in the range of care and support offers in Lambeth	I can choose support that I feel is suitable for me and my network from a range of different offers
	Style of Delivery	Support is delivered in an asset-based way	I receive support which builds upon my strengths, abilities and aspirations

(Continued)

Table 2.3 (Continued)

Big Three Outcomes	Outcome Area	Outcome	Person Statement
		Service users, families and carers feel involved in shared decision making about their care	My support networks and I feel respected as key partners in decision making
		Support and services are co-produced with people using services	I feel that I have an active and equal role in the design and delivery of services
Participation	Housing	Increase in the number of people living in stable and appropriate accommodation	I have a stable place to live which is suitable for me
	Employment	Increase in the number of people in education, training, volunteering or employment	I have a meaningful day-to-day role in society that suits me
	Social Networks	Increase in the number of people with strong social networks	I feel connected to and supported by other people in my community and networks
	Stigma reduction	Reduction in the stigma around mental health and increase understanding of mental wellbeing	I feel well informed and am comfortable to talk about mental health and wellbeing
	Workforce	Increase in staff ability to innovate and influence change	I feel empowered to influence change wherever I work in the system
		Increase in staff ability to do their jobs effectively	I have the necessary tools, resources and training to carry out my role effectively
	Finance	Investment is shifted towards early support	People receive early support that helps me to avoid reaching crisis point
		Increased investment in community organisations	People can choose support that I feel is suitable for me and my network from a range of different offers

Table 2.4 Cardiff and Vale Drug and Alcohol Service outcomes

Wellbeing outcomes	People feel (physically and psychologically) safe People have healthy relationships and relate to and connect positively to others People are able to positively participate in their communities People are mentally and physically healthy
Substance Misuse Specific Outcomes	People are aware of, and understand the consequences and risks of alcohol consumption and drug misuse Drug use and/or alcohol consumption is reduced
Workforce outcomes	The substance misuse workforce is skilled, capable, resilient, supported and empowered

Table 2.5 Cardiff and Vale Drug and Alcohol Service – service qualities

Person centred and strengths based	People using services are viewed as a whole person, with all of their needs and aspirations being supported. Supporting people to be in control of their journey through services. Flexible to people's individual circumstances. People's strengths, resilience, and resources are recognised and utilised.
Trauma informed	Recognising the impact of trauma, focusing on building and modelling healthy relationships, and working to the principles of psychologically informed environments; • Safety • Trustworthiness and transparency • Peer Support • Collaboration and mutuality • Empowerment, voice, and choice • Culture, historical, and gender issues
Including the support system around the person	Where possible, considering, supporting, and collaborating with the support system that surrounds the person using services including parents/carers, siblings, friends, community members.
Building resilience, not reliance	Identifying where additional resources can be brought in to complement services, for example; the time, skills, and resources of local citizens and businesses. • Supporting children, and people to access opportunities across Cardiff and the Vale, and beyond. • Building community connections.

Example 2 – The Cardiff and Vale Drug and Alcohol Service Alliance (CAVDAS)

For this alliance a set of outcomes was developed by an in-depth needs assessment. An outcome was defined as a meaningful and valued impact or change that occurs as a result of a particular activity or set of activities.

In discussions with frontline substance misuse workers and people with lived experience of using substance misuse services, it became clear that there were also various characteristics that people felt were important. These were described as 'service qualities'.

Both outcomes and service qualities are included in the evaluation of CAVDAS. Those involved in the Alliance report that they find them helpful in providing structure and focus.

DEVELOPING OUTCOMES

These examples show the value of describing outcomes from a range of perspectives. You can do this by reviewing the insights from any co-production and engagement work you have done in the past. Alternatively, you may want to do this as a group exercise as it's a great way to bring people together to share their own perspective and hear about the perspectives of others.

Workshop exercise – outcome development

Invite a range of people, starting with small mixed groups – preferably a good mix of residents, people who use services, those with lived experiences, frontline workers, managers and leaders from *different* organisations.

Tell everyone to think about their own perspective or role. You might need to say you give them permission to be selfish and narrowly focused on themselves. You can say it in a light-hearted way, but add that there is a reason to do this –namely, that you want to mix together all those individual perspectives, not just hear the dominant or expected ones.

You may also need to tell people not to think about how they would measure what they are thinking of. This is why the question I suggest below doesn't use the word 'outcome'. It is surprising how that word immediately makes some people think about metrics and evidence. Emphasise that you are want to get down what really matters to people, not what is or isn't measurable.

Pose the following question: 'Imagine a future where the alliance is successful. What would that look and feel like, what would that mean to you?' Ask people to write down one comment per sticky note. Do this individually for a few minutes.

Outcome 'snap'

Next, ask people to compare notes in their group and to collate their individual sticky note outcomes into piles where there are similarities. You can suggest they give each pile a name. These will end up being your outcome headings.

Then ask groups to compare with each other. As you go around the room, keep an eye on the themes and write them on a flipchart as headings. Then you can place the sticky notes against the relevant headings.

After the workshop you will need to ensure there is a manageable number of outcomes and, in translating many sticky notes to a table, you haven't lost important perspectives. The group will act as your sounding board when you send round the write-up and check your end result for fidelity and validity.

In summary, your common goal is key to understanding the alliance and everyone's commitment to it. The more it is created and defined from a range of perspectives, the stronger it will be.

Creating the four key elements – vision, purpose, objectives and outcomes – will take time and several iterations as you hear from others and keep refining and checking them. You will need a balance between aspiration and realism, big picture and detail, leaving enough room for the alliance itself to create and evolve the way it delivers on the shared vision.

Act in a certain way

The second building block is about the way people work with each other in the alliance, which we will break down to Alliance Principles, values and behaviours, and governance.

Alliance Principles

These are set for every alliance and are non-negotiable. They describe the alliance way of working, and represent the shared commitment everyone makes on being a member. I would argue that all collaborations need similar rules of engagement, but these are essential in a risk-sharing one where you cannot function without high levels of trust and reciprocity.

The Alliance Principles are:

1. to assume collective responsibility for all the risks involved in providing services
2. to make decisions on a 'best for people using services' basis;
3. to commit to unanimous, principle- and value-based decision making on all key issues;
4. to adopt a culture of 'no fault, no blame' among alliance participants, and to seek to avoid all disputes and litigation (except in very limited cases of wilful default);
5. to adopt open book accounting and transparency in all matters;
6. to appoint and select key roles on a best person basis; and
7. to act in accordance with the Alliance values and behaviours at all times.

Let's go through these in detail.

Principle 1 – Collective responsibility

Collective responsibility for all the risks is the fundamental difference between an alliance and most forms of partnership. It means that everyone takes responsibility for the whole rather than just their direct area of focus. From the first stages of design and planning through to delivery and further development, everyone has to understand the whole, and people share ideas and perspectives throughout.

One of the criticisms of some collaborations and partnerships is that people focus on the part that they are most familiar with. They therefore only see the whole from their perspective. Having collective responsibility for not just their bit, but everyone else's too; it moves everyone to a different place. The sharing of understanding and learning about others is a rich and rewarding aspect of being a member of an alliance. It means that everyone has a role not just in the delivery of the whole but in its planning, operation, overall co-ordination and, of course, its success or failure.

Framing this as shared responsibility for all the risks sounds scary. Taken literally, it could mean that I, in my organisation, have responsibility for all the risks that you, in your organisation, are holding.

In practice, it plays out in a pragmatic way. Each organisation will of course deliver and manage the risks for the part of the service or support that it is undertaking. If it is struggling for some reason – through, say staff shortage – then other organisations will say 'How can we help?' It is this collective responsibility that drives the well-described ethos of alliances, namely 'Your problem is my problem; your success is my success.' In one example, the Director of Operations of a large organisation said how liberating it had been to discover that they were able to discuss, and share with others, problems they felt they had been grappling with alone up until then.

Of course, the idea of shared financial risks is something that is often asked about by organisational Boards and Finance Directors thinking of joining an alliance. Our experience is that this leads to necessary and helpful conversations about risk-sharing and any mutual limitations that the alliance specifically wants to consider. These are not always easy conversations, but are a good test of the strength of the relationships in an alliance. Indeed, they often act to strengthen the relationships as the discussions proceed and conclude.

Principle 2 – Best for people

All major decisions made by the alliance members will be 'best for people using services'. This means that decisions must not be made on the basis of any member's self-interest. Decisions should not be 'best for my organisation'.

It is interesting to think about how many so-called collaborations are only collaborative up to a point. People are very happy to agree when the discussion is about generalities and doing the right thing; but when it comes to actually making changes, people find it very hard to move away from protecting their own organisation's interest first and foremost. This is natural and, in many ways, admirable. However, if it is getting in the way of doing the right thing for people then it becomes problematic.

In project alliances in other sectors, this principle is termed 'best for project'. It underlines that, once the alliance is formed and all members aligned, then decisions can be made as best for project. We have amended this to best for people using services as that most aptly describes how we should focus our decisions. We realise the term 'people using services' is not ideal as some alliances are not about services only, and there is a current movement that sees services as paternalistic and 'doing to'. However, it is the best term we've come up with to date. You are, of course, free to adopt a preferred term for your alliance, bearing in mind that it should always include the word 'people'.

In order for best for people or best for people using services to work you must be able to 'leave your organisation at the door'. Or, as someone once pointed out, leave your organisation's self-interest at the door because you should be bringing the resources, ideas and experience of your organisation into the room.

To be able to leave self-interest at the door, it is absolutely critical that all alliance members are aligned as success for the alliance must mean success for each of its members. If alignment is present, even if some decisions may seem to have a downside for some members, all members must be confident that, overall, they will be better able to meet their own aims. The alignment to their strategic aims and objectives should trump any short-term disruption from, for example, reduced or different staff mix or a change of activity on some of their sites.

In Alliance Leadership Team meetings, the big decisions need to be confirmed by each member present as being best for people using services. It is quite possible that there are different views on this. Some people may be thinking about people overall, others about a particular subset and others about individuals. This is normal and happens in all collaborations.

The important thing is to keep talking. Talk about these perspectives, look at the trade-offs, think about the short, medium and long term, look at compromises. All discussions are good and helpful for airing all the issues – and all the discussions will be focused on people, not on member organisations.

Principle 3 – Unanimous decision making

This is another main commitment for alliance members, and relates to all major decisions made by the Alliance Leadership Team. It means that, whatever the size of the organisation or its financial input in the alliance, it will have equal status around the table. This has been reassuring to smaller providers in some of our alliances, where they sit alongside larger organisations.

This principle is often questioned by people considering alliances. They are curious as to how it works in practice as most people's experience is of majority decision making and of one or two people around a table taking strongly held opposing views to the rest.

The unanimous principle links to the previous one about best for people using services. Differences of opinion should not be based on whether a decision is right or wrong for my organisation, so this removes much of the discord that can be present in other forms of partnerships.

Being focused on what is best for people should make it easier to come to unanimous agreements. If there are genuinely held views that the decision is not in the best interests of people, then those views need to be heard and resolutions found.

Resorting to a majority vote would mean that there is at least one person who does not think the decision is right, that it is not best for people. Majority voting may be expedient, but that is the problem. People should continue to discuss, debate and refine the decision. They should keep talking. Moving to a majority vote curtails this and can lead to things being rushed through without a sensible compromise or new approach being considered or taken.

Some people ask whether this principle is used by some as a veto. My response is that any alliance where the word 'veto' starts to be used, whether in private or in open meetings, is in the wrong place. It is in trouble. If people are raising this as the alliance forms, I would be seriously concerned that at least one alliance member is not really committed to the alliance way of working or that alignment has not been fully thought through. There is also a risk that one or more people agree to decisions just to keep things moving even if they secretly feel something is not best for people. This should be avoided as, again, it means that very legitimate views and perspectives are not being heard or considered.

Other aspects of unanimity are that decisions are based on principles and values. It can therefore be useful to refer to the Alliance Principles and values when there are disagreements about the best way forward. These reference points can sometimes help separate the issues for a difficult decision. They are also useful for decisions made by others in the alliance, but not in the Alliance Leadership Team, where you are aiming for collaborative rather than unanimous decisions.

Principle 4 – No fault, no blame

No fault, no blame

This is key for innovation and forms the first part of this principle. The driver for project alliancing in other sectors is innovation as well as collaboration. Having a no fault, no blame principle is effectively giving people permission to try new things. This was confirmed by a study by Lloyd-Walker and colleagues (2014) in Australia, who found that it was not enough to be collaborative. Alliances also need the ethos of no fault, no blame in order to be innovative.

If you think about it, everyone can collaborate to not change anything. It is unlikely but possible. Proactively saying no fault no blame means there is an expectation of trying new things, some of which may not work. If that is the case, then, after rewinding that change, the first question should be 'What can we learn from this?' This means that time is not wasted looking back as to whose idea it was, who is 'at fault' and who should pay for any redress.

Avoidance of disputes

Avoidance of disputes is the second part of the no fault, no blame principle. The dispute process for alliances is deliberately short. The Alliance Management Team is expected to prevent or quickly resolve disputes. If they are unable to, it then falls to the Alliance Leadership Team. If they cannot resolve the issues, the alliance ends. There is no protracted period of seeking external facilitation or arbitration as an alliance with a dispute requiring these is no longer functioning as such, and therefore should be wound up. I describe this as a sheer cliff edge; and, when everyone knows there is a cliff edge, they keep well away from it. This is a strong incentive to get on top of things quickly, to keep talking to find resolution and compromise as soon as possible.

It is important to stress that the principle of having no disputes does not mean there will be no disagreements. Differences of opinion, even strong ones, are healthy and a sign of people bringing different perspectives to a discussion. You don't want group think developing. The important thing is that there is respect between people, and that everyone is willing to listen, learn, change or amend their views and stick to the principle of best for people.

Principle 5 – Open book

Open and transparent reporting of finances and operations across the alliance is essential. Everyone is responsible and accountable for how the money is spent, so people should be able to see and, if necessary, interrogate each other's data.

One of the powerful changes I witnessed was from a developing alliance when people starting to compare their financial arrangements. Once everyone got past their initial reticence, they began to learn about the pressures others were facing and why things were as they were. They moved on quickly to have good conversations about how they might do things differently to make best use of the limited resources overall.

There is a slight caveat here relating to anti-competitive behaviour. Alliances must not become cartels and use their knowledge of each other's finances to gain advantages over others. Members should not use their inside knowledge of, for example, other alliance members' salaries, to position themselves more favourably if bidding for other work.

In our Alliance Agreements we include a clause on avoiding anti-competitive behaviour, which allows for the reporting of commercially sensitive information to the commissioner only. To date, as far as I am aware, this provision has not been needed.

Principle 6 – Best person basis

People working in an alliance are working for everyone. It should not matter which organisation they represent or who pays them. In other words, there is a sense of 'leave your organisation at the door'. This gives the alliance freedom to appoint or select the best people for any role. Say, for instance, you have a six-member alliance and five of them have one person each in key roles. If a sixth role then comes up you do not necessarily need to put someone in the role from the sixth organisation. The person appointed should be the best person for the role and, if that means it is another person from one of the other five members, then that is fine. Everyone is working for everyone.

Principle 7 – Values and behaviours

Each alliance creates its own set of values. These differ from Alliance Principles in that they usually reflect the specific set of services or people the alliance works with.

When you talk with people in long-standing alliances, it is clear that they are driven by values and relationships, some of which are named – for instance Lambeth's 'Alliance Way'. Others talk about how a focus on values has helped them through crises and challenges.

The values will be fundamental to the identity of the alliance. Although alliances are not legal entities, we refer to them as 'virtual organisations'. As such, they will need a visual identity, a brand, a sense of belonging for staff who may come from various organisations. A common set of values will be part of this.

In forming an alliance, we recommend carrying out an exercise to develop shared values, which might include collating those of the participant organisations or listening to people who use the services and the workforce.

Values, behaviours or both?

As you may know by now, I am not too precious about words. I have found that some people just use the word 'values', as in 'These are our organisation's values', whereas others make the point that you only know if someone is living values through their behaviours. This is a good point, and some organisations have a set of values and behaviours. It is for you, as an alliance, to decide what term(s) you prefer to use – which brings me to timing.

When to determine your values

Values should only be confirmed once the alliance is formed because you need all members to determine and finalise them. When we talk about the Commissioner as Owner creating the Alliance Mandate, we do not need to have a set of values. In fact, it would be wrong to do so. However, the Commissioner as Owner may want to describe its own values or those that it would expect to see. For instance, they may want the alliance to take a human rights approach or an asset-based one; or they may want to take the values from a relevant national report that contains a good co-produced set of values that might be adopted.

How to use the principles in practice

We advise new alliances to print out the principles, and even laminate them. They can then be taken to all alliance meetings and be referred to as needed. It helps to embed them in everyone's minds and ensure they are being lived in practice. We also recommend that the Alliance Leadership Team dedicate ten minutes at the end of every 2–3 meetings to ask themselves how well they are doing in demonstrating the principles.

At this stage, the idea is to make suggestions but to ensure you leave room for the alliance, once formed, to decide for itself.

Alliance governance

The last element of the Act in a Certain Way element of the alliance building block relates to governance: the way an alliance is run is key to implementing the Alliance Principles.

We look at the detail of alliance governance in Chapter 5, but here you will need an outline in order to help people decide whether or not they want to be part of your alliance. In our experience, people value reassurance that there is an established way of creating collaborative governance rather than leaving things unsaid or providing too much detail.

The Agreement

In our definition of an alliance – an agreement between two or more individuals or entities stating that the involved parties will act in a certain way in order to achieve a common goal – the agreement has primary place. The agreement for any collaboration needs to reflect the nature of the collaboration. If you have a relatively informal collaboration, you will not need an Alliance Agreement of the type we use. Many groups use a Memorandum of Understanding or similar to reflect their commitment to working together. However, a multiparty collaboration with sharing of responsibility and risk should be underpinned with a legal Alliance Agreement.

We go into this in detail in Chapter 4. Meantime, the main elements that prospective alliance members will want to know, such as contract term, funding allocation per year and other important parameters, can be added to your Alliance Mandate.

Summary

All collaborations or joint endeavours need clarity on the common goal. For alliances funded by large amounts of public money over several years, there must be a clear sense of what will be achieved if the collaboration is to be successful and how the alliance will work.

Working through a series of building blocks, you can create a short document with the key elements about your proposed alliance. Involving a range of people and perspectives will help build a strong Alliance Mandate.

You are now ready to go and talk to potential members about what they might bring to the alliance and their commitment to it.

Reference

Lloyd-Walker, B., Mills, A., & Walker, D. (2014). Enabling construction innovation: The role of a no-blame culture as a collaboration behavioural driver in project alliances. *Construction Management and Economics*, *32*(3), 229–245. https://doi.org/10.1080/01446193.2014.892629.

Case study 3

Future Pathways (2016–present)

The Future Pathways Alliance was launched in 2016 and operates across all of Scotland and beyond. It supports people who were abused or neglected as children while they were living in care in Scotland. Wherever the relevant people live now, whether in Scotland or anywhere else in the world, they can contact and receive support from Future Pathways to progress their personal outcomes. It provides co-ordination and support direct to individuals as well as outsourcing support and services from a range of other providers.

Creating the alliance

Future Pathways was formed as part of the Scottish Government's wider strategy to address the legacy of abuse in care in Scotland. A new approach was chosen to acknowledge the fact that the impacts of childhood abuse are individual and wide-ranging. The intention was to broaden the resources and support available to people, and to organise plans around personal outcomes so that the experience of support was integrated, trauma-informed and aligned with individual needs.

Initially the Scottish Government considered a consortium when it was recommissioning support for survivors. By mutual agreement with the chosen consortium, this was changed to an alliance, bringing a stronger sense of collective shared responsibility.

Progress of the alliance

Alongside the Scottish Government, there were three charity providers – Health in Mind, Penumbra Mental Health and the Mental Health Foundation, with NHS Greater Glasgow and Clyde joining after a few months. The three charities each took a different role. One is responsible for frontline delivery and acts as a banker for the Alliance; one is responsible for quality and learning; and the other was responsible for communication and engagement. However, this latter partner withdrew in 2021, and the communication element was incorporated into frontline delivery by mutual agreement of the remaining members.

Part of the funding is earmarked as a Discretionary Fund to be used for specific support for individuals following a conversation with one of the support co-ordinators to establish agreed personal outcomes. One of the highlights of this alliance is the devolved decision making about resources, right down to the personal level. In dialogue with an individual about their needs and preferences, the support co-ordinator can allocate funds of up to £1,000. Higher-value allocations are made by a panel of senior members of the Alliance who aim to make decisions quickly. This level of delegation, with appropriate and proportionate oversight, provides an excellent example of individual commissioning.

The Discretionary Fund is highly valued as support coordinators may also arrange for the purchase of services such as training courses, counselling and wellbeing therapies, among others that may be relevant.

In 2021, the Alliance was asked to develop a second national service, the Redress Support Service, which launched in December of that year, offering personalised support for people on their journey towards redress. Because of the commissioner's requirements, it was decided that operational separation was important, which led to the creation of two delivery teams instead of one Alliance Management Team. It was possible to design and launch that second service much faster and in a more structured way. Start-up was smooth, having incorporated all the learning from the first five years of operating Future Pathways.

What changed for people

When the Alliance was set up, it was estimated that about 145 people might register in a given year. In fact, registration rates have been 2–3 times higher. As of January, 2024, more than 2,500 people were registered, and growing numbers of people are saying how important and valued this work is. A key message from a scoping study undertaken in 2018 was that the experience of a positive relationship was as transformative as the provision and co-ordination of support. The resources are, of course, important – but how they are offered is even more so.

Alliance members are motivated to get it right for people recognising that they have been poorly served by professionals and services in the past. There is a shared aim of transforming how support is offered, smoothing the way when multiple services are needed and centring the principles of trauma-informed practice in all aspects of the work. The diversity of needs means a collaborative approach is essential.

Individuals comment that it feels like 'finally people are listening and understanding'. There is evidence of the importance of a Support Co-ordinator in convening support around the individual and encouraging others to understand that person's needs and question their own processes and practices.

There are powerful stories of people who have benefited from Future Pathways' tailored support, whether direct, facilitated or commissioned. The impact of this alliance can cascade across many areas of their lives.

Full reports on the Alliance's progress against set outcomes are available at https://future-pathways.co.uk/stepping-stones/.

3 Alliance members

The members of an alliance are essential elements for success, so it is critical to select the right members: people and organisations who are committed to the same shared purpose and the alliance way of working. Selection of those organisations with the best alignment, capability and capacity is therefore key. The way you go about identifying members will set the tone for what you hope will be a successful and long-lasting collaboration. Prospective alliance members will be alongside you for many years as trusted colleagues and partner organisations.

In this chapter we will look at different ways alliance members are selected and some of the key considerations, taking the perspective of both commissioners and provider organisations. At the end of the chapter you will have a good sense of how to decide on alliance members, whether for your own organisation or those you would like alongside.

Public sector commissioning

Identification of member organisations for a public sector funded alliance must meet the national public laws governing commissioning. This includes the regulation of public sector contracts under procurement law, and public sector grants and other subsidies under subsidy control law.

Some people think that choosing an alliance means they don't have to go to through an objective, open and transparent commissioning process. This is not the case. As you consider how you will identify alliance members you will need to fulfil your duty to be transparent, demonstrating public good, value for money and fair treatment.

The commissioning process may or may not include a regulated procurement. However, despite common perceptions, procurement does not have to mean competition. There is an excellent summary of different options in *The Art of the Possible in Public Procurement* by Frank Villeneuve-Smith and Julian Blake (2016).

DOI: 10.4324/9781003511809-3

There are potentially some very specific circumstances where you can move from an existing collaboration to a formal alliance contract. We will start with these and then move on to open-market procurement processes.

Building on an existing collaboration

Many places have very good collaborative forums, groups and even delivery partnerships. Moving to the next level for an existing collaboration seems to make sense. You have worked well together and now want to share more responsibility, maybe including decisions about funding. So why not just turn this into an alliance?

It is entirely understandable that people want to build on existing collaborations rather than throw everything up in the air with a formal process. You may want to avoid disrupting relationships and all the potential additional work in preparing tender documentation and evaluating bids.

However turning an existing collaboration into an alliance is not just a question of changing the name. There are critical differences and you need to work through these to ensure every member of your new alliance is fully committed to the new way of working. It is far from an easy option.

An alliance is not a meeting

An alliance means a whole way of working and commitment to collaboration that has implications extending to each member organisation. This differs greatly from most collaborations in health and care.

An alliance entails shared risks, integrated governance and collective responsibility for the delivery and distribution of public money, so it is likely to be different from the way your collaboration has operated so far.

Most collaborative forums, while great for exchanging ideas and developing new initiatives together, have a relatively voluntary and flexible input from any one organisation. Typically, there is a core of actively engaged members, both individuals and organisations, and then others who attend less frequently or have more peripheral involvement. This probably works well and fits the purpose.

Moving to an alliance would mean each member shares full responsibility, including financial, for a whole set of support and services. Each one needs to be equally committed to making the alliance successful. Each organisation's own specific funding, activities and workforce, as far as they relate to alliance activity, may need to change over time as decided by you and your fellow alliance members collectively. Decisions are no longer for the organisation on its own.

This is quite a stark difference. It is certainly not just a case of saying we are changing the name of our meetings from 'collaborative forum' to 'alliance'. There are a series of considerations when thinking about creating an alliance from an existing collaboration.

Numbers

Your collaborative forum may have a large number of participants and invitees. Attendance and commitment will be mainly voluntary. There may be some very active partners and others who are less so. As discussed in the previous chapters, we recommend that an alliance – as a formal, contracted, risk- and responsibility-sharing collaboration – should have no more than eight members. This is because equity between members and shared decision making become more difficult with more members. You may need to consider how you will move from a larger group to a smaller one, who will decide and how you handle the changes without impacting on the trust and relationships you have built up.

New entrants, new perspectives

An existing collaboration may already have a range of perspectives from various people, but there may be others who could make a positive contribution that no one yet knows about. You will not want to miss out on talent and expertise in an organisation that has not been part of your existing collaboration.

Alliances can have 5-, 7- or even 10-year contract terms, so you are potentially closing out others from having an opportunity to be part of the alliance for several years. There may be organisations not yet party to the collaboration that perceive, rightly or wrongly, that there is a cartel, a closed shop, and they have no chance to participate. You have a duty to be fair and transparent with everyone, not just those you are already working with. It will be important to check you are not missing out on fresh thinking as well as protecting yourself and your future alliance from accusations of cronyism and stitch-ups.

Nature of the collaboration

An alliance with the formal delegation of public funds and responsibility for co-ordination and delivery is a very different proposition to a forum that meets to share ideas and learning and plan specific, time-limited projects. Member organisations need to be present at all key meetings. There needs to full commitment to the alliance, its purpose and objectives and shared responsibility for ensuring delivery. Without this understanding and commitment from every member, the alliance will struggle to be successful.

Relationship reset

Following from the previous point, an alliance usually requires a different form of relationship between all parties. I often hear that an existing collaboration has achieved much but there have also been delays or lack of progress on some issues. There may have been a lot of talk but not much action.

Moving to an alliance will signify a change in relationships as it will have responsibilities that an informal, voluntary group can never have. The phrase a colleague uses is 'hard money contract', which is very different to the more informal collaborations and learning partnerships that we usually see.

One of the positive reasons for going through an open procurement process is that the Commissioners as Owners are saying that this is what we want to achieve for people, this is how we want everyone to work together. If you are interested in being part of that, apply to be part of the alliance; if not, don't. It is a reset of relationships and way of working, and is harder to achieve when trying to segue from an existing collaboration to an alliance.

Speed of change

I am often asked how long it takes to procure an alliance via open tender. I say at least a year from starting to pull together the documentation, getting internal approval, publishing the tender documents, receiving bids, evaluation, negotiating, confirming preferred bidder and mobilising prior to launch.

If asked how long it takes an existing group to morph into an alliance, I say 18 months as a minimum, based on experience of seeing that you can only go at the speed of the most reluctant partners. There is a lot to do and a reluctant partner will, consciously or unconsciously, dictate the timescales for making decisions, getting approval and finalising paperwork. I have seen how delays cause frustration and prevent the building of trust. You may therefore need to think carefully about starting the alliance with willing and committed partners and adding others later.

Expectations and relationships reset

If you have worked through the issues above and are happy to proceed to turn an existing collaboration into an alliance, you will need to plan how to get everyone to move to the new way of working. This won't happen overnight or at a single meeting; it will take several months or even years, and you will find there are times when things seem to be going backwards. I have seen this many times in collaborations. People are very happy to meet and talk about a high-level common vision – easy to agree, easy to find shared ground. However, the minute you start talking about finances and moving money around, some people will say they did not know this was up for discussion. They might leave the table, metaphorically let's say, and you may need to spend time and energy persuading them to come back.

You manage to do that and continue the discussions. You then introduce the idea of a legal agreement and ask them to sign. I can guarantee you will again get that scattering effect. It doesn't matter how much you have all agreed previously – that this is the direction you are going in and these are the timelines – when the crunch comes at least one person or organisation will say they did not know a particular aspect was part of the deal.

This may sound cynical but it is surprisingly common. That says to me that it is normal behaviour; we hear what we want to hear and see what we want to see. It is asking a lot for people to change their established ways of working and commit their organisation and their colleagues to a collaboration where they will lose some autonomy and unilateral decision making power.

My advice is to plan for these backward steps as well as doing all you can to avoid them. Communication is key – having a compelling narrative and making sure everyone has the chance to hear it, shape it and discuss it with others. It also means listening, really listening, for small hints of concern and resistance. We recommend a stepped process over several months, based on setting up shadow arrangements as soon as possible that will allow everyone to be in the room and part of the operational decision-making as you progress through to a full alliance.

Step 1 – Confirm the mandate for the alliance

The members of the existing collaboration are likely to be ideally placed to help you shape the vision and objectives from which you can construct the Alliance Mandate. However, you are now moving from a collectively agreed statement to a contractual form. Each member organisation will need to formally accept the mandate and confirm that they are willing to be an alliance member, collectively responsible for delivering it.

It will take time for each organisation to get approval from their governing bodies to proceed. There may be some elements, especially regarding funding allocations, that need negotiation prior to approval. The commissioners will need to demonstrate they have considered the implications of procurement law and fulfilled their obligations within it.

Step 2 – Preparation to launch a Shadow Alliance

We advise a certain period of time, usually 3–6 months, where the alliance operates in shadow form as this allows people to get used to new ways

Figure 3.1 Moving from an existing collaboration to an alliance

of working. The Shadow Alliance Leadership Team should be made up of members who will form the full alliance. They can start to move from a mono-organisational focus to a 'one-team' multi-organisational approach. They will collectively create and own all the mobilisation and delivery plans: operations delivery, communications, workforce, quality improvement plans and others.

The Shadow Alliance Leadership Team will govern, lead and create the infrastructure and appointments needed to run a collaborative, co-ordinated set of support and services. To prepare a Shadow Alliance a few things need to be done:

- Confirm each member, checking they have the right capabilities, capacity, commitment and alignment.
- Confirm each member's board or equivalent has approved their inclusion and agreed to delegate authority for their representative on the team.
- Where necessary, undertake due diligence on members to confirm their financial health and sustainability.
- Ensure that all members sign up to the Alliance Mandate and/or the Terms of Reference for the Shadow Alliance Leadership Team.

This last point will reveal whether any potential alliance member will find it hard to sign the Alliance Agreement. In a sense you are forcing the issue so you can identify whether or not the member organisations are really ready to move to a more risk-sharing type of collaborative working. It is far better to know this now than at a later stage, just before the launch of the full alliance. You will have time to address any issues that may keep that member organisation in the alliance – or not.

We find that getting together to clarify all these elements can be helpful. An awayday with two or three key people from each organisation can suffice, ideally a mix of those who will be closely involved and others who may have a more peripheral role, either at board level or in another part of the organisation. We include:

- introductions and getting to know you time
- clarification of the Alliance Mandate and Alliance Principles
- our shared values, hopes, fears and concerns
- next steps.

Step 3 – Launch Shadow Alliance

Once the Shadow Alliance begins operation, it has three main areas of activity: governance; management, co-ordination and infrastructure; and planning.

GOVERNANCE

The Shadow Alliance Leadership Team will meet regularly and start putting into practice the Alliance Principles, including best for people and unanimous decision making. On a practical note, they will need to appoint a Chair and decide on the frequency of meetings and the terms of reference. At some point, formal reporting to the commissioners on Alliance performance will begin. We recommend starting this as soon as possible even if there are initially more gaps than content.

MANAGEMENT, CO-ORDINATION AND INFRASTRUCTURE

An interim Alliance Manager will need to be assigned or recruited. Other functions – for instance, administration support, communications, data and analytics and finance – will also be required. Whether these are full-time roles or part of someone's remit in one of the member organisations will depend on the size and scope of the alliance. Some Shadow Alliances have interim or Shadow Alliance Management Teams. Again, this is a chance for people to get used to working together in a more structured collaborative way, focused on the Alliance's vision and objectives.

PLANNING

A number of plans may need finalising or creating, concerning, for example:

- service delivery
- implementation
- workforce
- communication – including branding and websites
- quality improvement.

Compilation of a Services Operations Manual will commence, although this may take several iterations and many months to complete (see Chapter 4).

Step 4 – Prepare for launch of full alliance

By now, the move toward the alliance will be in full swing, and hopefully people are seeing the benefits of working collaboratively, sharing ideas and challenges. The final elements needed to form a full alliance are shared financial responsibility and risk.

On the commissioning side, the mechanisms for pooling budgets and funds will need to be completed and agreed. On the providers' side, there are practicalities such as identifying a host banker, if required, and setting up reporting and assurance arrangements. Any risk-sharing will need to be discussed and agreed.

The Alliance Agreement will then need to be finalised and signed. This includes the schedules on scope, finance, performance, data-sharing and service standards. This step could take considerable time: people in member organisations often have a lot of questions and challenges as the reality and deeper understanding of what is being proposed sinks in.

Step 5 – Launch the alliance

You are there! You have a group of organisations that are equally committed to working collectively to achieve your vision. This should be marked in some way. This could be anything from a press release to an internal gathering of personnel from the various member organisations to hear about the alliance, to a staged signing ceremony at an event with a wide guest list. However it is marked, the alliance is now live and ready to go.

Procurement

I am not a procurement specialist but have been lucky enough to have worked alongside such professionals as we have developed our alliances. The information here is based on my personal experience of alliance developments. It is very important to seek appropriate specialist procurement advice as you develop your alliance for your specific context.

Procurement of an alliance is no different to any other procurement in that the same national legal and statutory considerations apply. The route you take will depend on these and your local circumstances. In the UK there is a clear duty to be fair and transparent. This is also true for most countries, even if terms and processes differ.

Alliances are all about collaboration, so it can seem strange to have to go through a formal process that entails an element of competition or judgement in order to create an alliance. There is no doubt that procurement can be stressful and time-consuming for both commissioners and providers. On the other hand, it is the start of deep and longstanding relationships, so it is important to ensure that you and your potential partners are the right fit. The trick is to make any competition about who can be the best at collaboration, not a race to the bottom on price.

Collaborate to compete; compete to collaborate.

The overall aim of the procurement process is to end up with the right members for your alliance. All parties need to be convinced that they are the right combination, that all are equally committed to the alliance's purpose and outcomes and to its way of working. You should be confident that, collectively, you have the right skills and capabilities to deliver. How you go about the procurement process can also signal your commitment to your new roles as commissioner of an alliance and how you want to work in co-production, drawing on the expertise of people with lived experiences.

Alliance member procurement in other sectors

In learning about alliances in other sectors, I was struck by how they go about identifying members. In its purest form, the procurement process involves testing organisational fit and commitment to collaboration and innovation. There is no testing of design and delivery models or costs until the members have been selected and the Alliance Agreement signed. To explain this in more detail, Fig 3.2 is based on a process shared with me by my brother's Australian business consultancy, Alchimie Pty.

You will see that the starting point is experience in collaboration and innovation, and these are further tested in selection workshops. It is only once the preferred group is selected that the commissioners carry out commercial alignment, and even then this is about the principles of the commercial framework rather than financial plans and costs. Once there is commercial alignment – that is, the principles and outline of remuneration, gainshare and painshare are agreed – then the Alliance Agreement is signed.

The next phase, taking several weeks or months, concerns target outturn costs (TOC), when the alliance project teams work out design details and estimated costs. A key benefit of the collaborative approach to TOC development is open and robust conversations about risk. Since everyone shares in all risks, there is a strong incentive for such conversations in order to agree on appropriate contingencies. As clients want to drive prices down and contractors want plenty of safety factors, the model needs to have the 'right' target costs.

Too often in lump sum bid forms of contracting, the contractor is less informed about the risks and faces competitive pressure to under-price

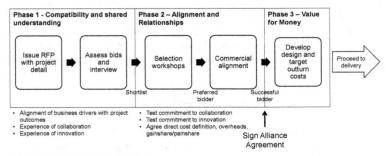

RFP = Request for Proposal (Invitation to Tender)

Figure 3.2 Procurement process for project alliances

risk, which can lead to claims if the risks materialise. By having the owner, designer and contractor sharing perspectives about risk, the robustness of the TOC is increased. The costs and design details are presented to the owners for approval, and there may be various iterations; but if the final version is deemed unsuitable and cannot be agreed upon, the alliance is terminated and the process then recommences with the second-highest bidder.

This sequence makes complete sense if you look at procurement as a process for choosing the right partners first and foremost. Doing this thoroughly means that the selected group of organisations and people are trusted to create innovative, affordable plans to deliver the objectives and outcomes set for the alliance. It means that the procurement process is not asking for providers to create a costed delivery model in order to be selected. They only do that once the alliance is formed and it is a shared collaborative endeavour. Unsuccessful bidders will not have wasted time, often many months, creating hypothetical delivery plans which are then discarded.

This approach to procurement is accepted in countries that have similar laws and regulations to the UK (such as Australia), yet it is not a practice that our UK alliances have followed. One reason may be that they are long term, so there is more possibility of changes in personnel and organisational focus before the end of the contract life. Therefore, focusing procurement solely on relationships and organisational fit may be too narrow.

In addition, in the UK there is typically a large percentage of evaluation criteria on finances and costs, and there is often reluctance to move away from this. While there are other ways to ensure value for money and careful use of public finances, competitive tendering on price is long established.

Group bids or individual bids

We strongly advise that you invite bids from groups of providers rather than inviting organisations to bid individually and then choosing ones to be the provider members of your alliance. If you were to do this, you would keep all the bidders in competition with each other right up to the contract being awarded. You would then only be able to start the collaboration and team-building after that. Also, each provider will have no say over who their fellow provider members will be. Any difficulties and conflicts will, quite rightly, be laid firmly at your door.

It is therefore much better to invite group bids. Here provider organisations form themselves into groups that immediately start collaborating on their bid. They go through team formation and building, united by a common purpose, namely winning the bid. The providers purposely choose who is and isn't in the group, so they will be invested in each other. They will check the alignment between themselves and consider how the individual members of the group can combine to provide a strong, attractive offer.

Some providers may be involved in more than one bid, and it is entirely up to them and the other organisations whether or not to permit this. They will want to create Non-Disclosure Agreements (NDAs) or similar to manage any conflict of interest and confidentiality issues. It may feel uncomfortable for commissioners not to be able to influence who is in each group. It will be an early test of the trust you need to demonstrate as you develop your alliance.

Sample Procurement processes

In our alliances to date we have used open procedures, competitive dialogue, and variations of these. The following three examples show how these were applied.

Alliance in practice – Lambeth Living Well Network

This alliance has responsibility for most adult mental health support and services in the London borough of Lambeth, including prevention, early intervention and support as well as clinical and inpatient services for individuals aged 18–65 (but excluding addiction services). It incorporated the earlier Integrated Personalised Support Alliance (IPSA) and the Living Well Network Hub and related services. These had been running for about two years, and had already helped reduce the number of referrals to secondary care services while increasing the number of people given support.

Lambeth Council and Clinical Commissioning Group (CCG) had a positive experience of alliancing with IPSA and were keen to spread the alliance way of working to other areas. IPSA provided services and support to people with severe and enduring mental illness. The aim of the Living Well Network Alliance was to provide almost all services and support for working-age adults with mental distress.

It was important for the new alliance to be open, transparent and fair to all while recognising the strengths and commitment of the existing group of IPSA members. A suitable process was selected. The council and the CCG issued an open 'Expression of Interest' notice to test market interest in their proposition from groups of providers that would consider bidding once the invitation to tender was issued. Three submissions were received, but only one was credible as two were from single, small organisations. The credible submission was from existing members of IPSA.

It was therefore clear that there was no viable market, so the commissioners decided to proceed to direct negotiations with the remaining group that had expressed an interest. A Voluntary Ex-Ante Transparency

(VEAT) notice explaining the move to direct negotiation was published, giving a further ten days for anyone to challenge the decision. No one did.

This approach allowed the commissioners to be fair, transparent and proportionate. The negotiation moved to a shared task of developing a robust delivery and financial plan for the first two years of the contract. This took several months and numerous iterations as the funding allocations and the ambition for change needed to be reconciled. The procurement process was therefore able to move away from finding alternative providers to finding the best solutions for delivery and co-ordination within the available budget.

The whole process had been considered carefully to ensure we were being fair to all. If there had been more than one viable response to the initial Expression of Interest notice, we would have proceeded to a call for competition. In the event, we proceeded to direct negotiation. The VEAT notice gave extra reassurance that the commissioners were not disadvantaging others.

Alliance in practice – The Prevention Alliance

For their alliance, Stockport Council decided on an open procurement procedure. The council's procurement and legal advisers helped adapt standard processes and templates to accommodate some of the key features of an alliance, such as the testing of collaboration in selection processes and the drafting of contracts.

Market information sessions and dedicated (independent) market support were arranged to prepare the market for the changes ahead, and in January 2015 an invitation to tender was issued. Bids were invited from groups of providers that could demonstrate they had an innovative model for generic prevention services. They also had to show how they would meet the outcomes set by the council. The selection process included scoring around meeting the outcomes and delivery competence. Face-to-face evaluation included scenarios and presentations to test commitment to collaboration and innovation.

Scenario workshops

We used scenario workshops for the first time in this procurement process, and have since undertaken them many times. They are our version of the selection workshops used in other sectors.

Bidding groups are invited to sessions and given a number of scenarios to work through. Trained observers mark their discussions and interactions using objective competence scorecards. The scores are then collated and moderated. The scenario sessions allow evaluation of the groups' commitment to collaboration in a way that written responses can never do. We usually allocate 10 per cent of the overall score for the bids to collaboration and test this through these face-to-face workshops.

Alliance in practice – Glasgow Alliance to End Homelessness

I am including this example here even though the Glasgow Alliance unfortunately ended early because of a series of circumstances following its launch (see Case Study 7). However, its procurement process was, in my view, a good one as it had strong involvement of people with lived experience and used a competitive dialogue procedure well.

This alliance was set up to provide accommodation, personal support and routes into employment for people who were homeless or at risk of homelessness. Its objectives included: ending rough sleeping; preventing homelessness and alleviating its impact; reducing the length of time people spent in temporary accommodation; minimising repeat homelessness; and helping tenants who were formerly homeless maintain their tenancies.

A co-produced, city-wide review of homelessness services was facilitated by Glasgow Homeless Network (now Homeless Network Scotland), where the need for a more collaborative way of working was established. Alliance contracting seemed to be a good way to achieve this and move away from the piecemeal approach in place at the time.

Glasgow Health and Social Care Partnership were committed to creating the alliance very early on, and spent time finalising the prospectus, drawing up the legal documents and planning the procurement. A competitive dialogue procedure was chosen as this would allow refinement of the delivery and other plans as procurement proceeded. The invitation to tender was issued in May 2019 and a number of dialogue sessions scheduled at 4–6-week intervals, with the final decision made in December and formally accepted in February 2020.

One of the dialogue sessions was dedicated to scenario workshops, where observers included several people with lived experience of homelessness who had been specially trained for the sessions and to be part of the evaluation panel (see Chapter 7 for more detail).

The council's legal advisers were closely involved in all stages of the competitive dialogue process as it was important to demonstrate fairness and equitability at all times. The dialogue meetings with each bidding group needed to be balanced between giving individual feedback to each group and common overall aims. Once the preferred bidding group was announced, mobilisation commenced and the Alliance went live in April 2020.

These three examples show the different procurement routes used in the formation of some of the alliances up and running in the UK. All used the route that was most appropriate and deliverable in their context. Competitive procedures with negotiation, competitive dialogue or the new competitive flexible procedure proposed in the UK allow for two-way conversations during the procurement process. While these can take longer than open procedure procurements, they fit well with the alliance ethos and way of working.

We have not yet used innovation partnerships, a model introduced in the UK in the Public Contracts Regulations 2015. While the initial take-up of this approach has not been widespread, experience is growing. It is certainly another alternative to traditional approaches to competitive tendering for services for people (Veitch & Bland, 2023).

Co-production in evaluation

The evaluation of groups bidding to be members of an alliance will be strengthened by including the voices and perspectives of people with relevant lived experience. It is also an opportunity to demonstrate your commitment to putting people front and centre of your alliance. There are many ways in which people with these lived experiences can help make it successful. One is by taking part in the selection of its members. It is fairly standard practice to include someone with direct experience of the support and services you are asking your alliance to co-ordinate and manage to be part of an evaluation panel. This is often one individual who is asked to take part.

This is the least that would be expected and, like in the Glasgow example, some organisations go further. When done well, this can make a big difference and will add to the validity of the process and the final decision.

Procurement documents

We strongly encourage you to think of the procurement process as a showcase for how you are changing as a commissioner. You are looking for people and organisations to work alongside for several years – the start of new relationships. The style and language you use in your procurement documents will therefore be an opportunity to demonstrate your new approach. Of course, you will need some of the standard documentation developed by your procurement and legal advisers, but you use them in a way that creates a different feel.

Each organisation will have its own policies and paperwork for procurement, but all will have some variation on the three main documents needed at the start of the process:

- a prospectus or specification – details of what you want for your target audience and how you want the whole system to work;
- the invitation to tender– instructions on how to bid;
- the Alliance Agreement – the legal document that will underpin the alliance (see Chapter 4).

The prospectus

We tend to use the term 'prospectus' here rather than 'specification' to differentiate it from the usual typical specifications that detail the services and support to be offered, opening hours, staffing levels, etc.

All those familiar with public sector procurement will know that most specifications are not shining examples to follow when we want to encourage and engage applications for innovative and long-term relationships. A service specification will typically be a lengthy Word document set out in numbered headings, subheadings and paragraphs, and 'public sector speak'. There will be pages of background and references to strategies, national policies and guidance, so it can sometimes take a while to find what is actually being asked for.

Other sectors may use a much stronger marketing approach in order to find great organisations that think innovatively. They want to create a sense of excitement and possibility for the future. Their materials include well-produced brochures about their aims, and they put money and effort into how they want to be seen in order to attract the best.

I'm not always a fan of glossy brochures, but I realise that we could sometimes do with a bit of this approach. Think of ones you have seen, either in print or online: come to our school, join our courses, buy our properties, our holidays. These say what they are all about and what you need to do to apply, but in ways that grab the attention and give the feel and ethos of what they are about. We now have good examples of colourful, well-designed, professionally typeset prospectuses from alliances in Camden and Durham, among others.

CONTENT

Your prospectus needs to set the scene, the drivers for change, and describe your ambitions for people. It should have enough information for those outside the area or unfamiliar with your developments to date to enable them to decide whether they are interested in and want to find bidding partners to link up with.

Importantly, the text should tell a story; it should hang together and not be a set of disjointed sections with facts, figures and graphs that leave people having to work out what they need to respond to. If you have created a good mandate for your alliance with clear vision, purpose, objectives and outcomes, this will form the basis of your prospectus. From my experience, below are a few do's and don'ts.

INTRODUCTION – DON'T WAFFLE, GET STRAIGHT TO THE POINT

A short introduction following your title page should explain what you are asking for and why. You will be expanding on this later in the document, so just the essentials are needed here, as in this example from County Durham's prospectus:

> Durham County Council is developing a collaborative approach to a range of support services for mental health wellbeing for people across Durham County, including prevention, early identification and recovery support.
>
> We are eager to receive inventive bids that mirror our commitment to prevention, early identification and recovery support and are based on collaborative working, championing service users' voices, and codesign and co-production.
>
> We want to hear from forward-looking providers, be they, statutory, community and voluntary sector or private sector. We are especially interested in user led and community based organisations, and we are keen to hear from any groups of providers who can demonstrate to us that they are committed to improving the lives and experiences of people with mental health needs.
>
> We want to bring together people using services, providers and commissioners to create ideas and plans for improving mental health services and support in County Durham.
>
> This is an ambitious, whole system approach, requiring commitment and determination to achieve positive outcomes for people across County Durham.

This helps people understand from the start what the issue is all about. It comes across as positive, ambitious and exciting, which sets the tone.

BACKGROUND INFO – PUT IT AT THE BACK

An academic or research paper will typically follow an abstract, background, methods, results and interpretation format. We do this for board or committee papers too, putting the demographics, strategy development, who we consulted with and when at the start of the document.

The trouble is, people are not that interested in this information, and instead want to get to the heart of the matter as soon as possible. Your introduction generated interest, so don't kill it off with a few of pages of stats and doom-mongering about how bad things are. Of course, those unfamiliar with your locality will want that information, so you can put it in appendices or in an accompanying technical information document or separate pack.

DRIVERS FOR CHANGE – DON'T DENIGRATE WHAT YOU ALREADY HAVE

Moving to a different way of working may mean, by definition, that not all is well with how you are working now. You might want to take that further and say that current support and services are not good enough, maybe even poor or failing.

I would advise against too much criticism of the status quo and the current providers of support and services. There will always be pockets of good and even great practice. There will always be excellent and committed people wanting to do the right thing, but with the system getting in the way.

A narrative that is about having some good things but not always co-ordinated well or able to shine or something similar will mean you are not disenfranchising or insulting a large part of your market before you have started. Talk instead about drivers such as technological advances and wanting to do more to put people in control. That way the reasons for change are more positive.

SIGNAL WHAT TYPE OF BIDS YOU WANT BUT REMAIN FLEXIBLE

Your procurement and legal advisers will rightly tell you that you cannot dictate who can apply. You cannot say you only want community and voluntary sector providers or only local ones; but you can hint at the type of bids you hope to attract. For example, you can say that diversity of alliance members is important, that you expect the bidding group to include organisations of varying size and capability. You could say you expect some to have good local knowledge, but probably shouldn't go further than that.

We advocate hinting at the numbers you expect in a bidding group. Working on the basis that your alliance should have no more than eight members (including the commissioners), you can say that you are looking for groups of between four and seven, for example. The important thing is that these are read as suggestions only, and that anyone is free to submit a bid.

LANGUAGE, STYLE AND TONE

Language matters greatly, so demonstrating this in the first public document about your alliance is very important. Try to use language that will be understood by all, not jargon or service speak. It can be hard to write for a general audience if you are accustomed to writing for boards and committees, using a certain type of language and phraseology, as well numerous acronyms and abbreviations.

Writing in plain English and avoiding commonly used shorthand that has crept into professional spheres shows you are able to step outside your role and think of people as, well, people. We have all heard people say that they feel excluded by the terminology that is used in meetings. If they cannot understand it, how can they engage with it and feel like equal parties?

Several years ago when I was working in what is now NHS England, the NHS Director of Human Resources, who had recently arrived from the private sector, asked me what was meant by an acronym I had just used. To my eternal shame I couldn't remember. There are so many abbreviations in the NHS (itself an abbreviation of course), often three-letter ones, that we end up using them so often we forget what they stand for. This occasion was an important lesson for me.

I later worked with a fantastic communications team that included some ex-journalists, and learnt that the only acceptable abbreviations are NHS and GP. Even saying the full term and introducing the acronym or abbreviation that you then use in the rest of the document should only be used for very long and unwieldy terms.

FOCUS ON PEOPLE NOT SERVICES

Being people- rather than service-centred makes for a big difference in tone. Below is a sentence from material used for developing a prospectus. It involved support and services for children and young people with special educational needs or disabilities (SEND), and contained a list of the priorities for the proposed alliance, including this example for early help:

Through intervening early, either in the early years or when a need is identified, and delivering a co-ordinated approach for families.

We changed this to:

Where a child or young person is identified as having or thought to have a special educational need or disability, there will be early, co-ordinated support which is tailored to the child and their circumstances.

I admit this is still a bit clunky, but now we are clearly talking about what a child or young person and their family can expect. The subject – grammatically as well as in your thinking – is the child and young person.

This matters for demonstrating your thinking both now and later down the line. There will be difficult times in any alliance, and being able to come back and consider you are doing through the eyes and words of those you are there to support and work alongside will be very helpful as you work though any interpersonal or interorganisational difficulties. It allows you to go back to your common goal and why you wanted to be part of an alliance in the first place.

The invitation to tender

It always amuses me that we call bid documents 'invitations'. When I look at the standard format that some organisations use, it's hard to think of anything less inviting. The worst examples are pages of poorly typeset boxes, bold and capitals telling you what to do and what not to do. Of course, we can't get away from the fact that we need to give bidders information about the process, and some of that may need to be written in formal or even legal language.

We also need bidders to provide information about themselves as businesses and their suitability as the partners and collaborators we seek. The evaluation criteria you apply and the questions you ask are your opportunity to select the best and help make sure your alliance is a success. At the end of the procurement process you should be confident you have a top-rate group of alliance members, individually as well as collectively. To get there, the minimum you need is one really good bid. The question is what does that look like? How will you know?

Regardless of which procurement procedure you are following, alongside technical questions about finance, insurance and so on, you should usually devise some questions to test whether the bidding group has the right capabilities to deliver on your vision and achieve the outcomes you seek. Yes, there will be differences between the responses you are looking for from bidding groups in an open procedure like an invitation to tender and those from an invitation to participate in dialogue. But, throughout, your questions and evaluation criteria should align with your vison, objectives and outcomes.

You can also use the bid responses to build the delivery and other plans for the alliance, meaning that much of the work on these will already have been done by the time you know your preferred bidding group.

Evaluation criteria

Let's be honest, we've all been there. We write up some evaluation criteria headings and create a table with some percentages down the side and make them total 100. You might include standard ones from your organisation – for instance 30 per cent for finance, 10 per cent for social value. If there is time, we circulate this to our teams and ask for comments, and then finalise. Next we write some questions under each heading, which become the ones the bidders have to address in their written responses.

An alternative is to take a more collaborative and developmental approach, one that builds from the bottom up. By doing so you will create a much stronger validated set of evaluation criteria and questions that will stand you in good stead for the future. Yes, it may take a little more time, but not much – a single two-hour workshop should suffice. You will also get the added benefit of spending time with colleagues and partners who will be key to getting the selection of alliance members right.

Workshop exercise – evaluation criteria development

Assemble a range of people who can help define what 'good' looks like. This will include people in your team and organisation as well as expert advisers – that is, people with lived experiences. As this concerns procurement and how the bids will be evaluated, you must be sure everyone understands about confidentiality and non-disclosure.

- Ask everyone to write down, in their own words, what would tell them that a particular bidding group is the 'right' one. Use a prompt, such as 'I will know this group is the best one if . . .' Don't restrict people to what they might read in a written response; be open to other ways people describe what they want to see, feel or hear.
- Now compare responses and group them under themes or headings. Discuss them, tweak them and finally agree your overall set.
- The next step is to weight the headings. Ask which ones people feel are most important and which can be secondary. You may need to use a voting system with stickers if there is a lot of debate.
- You should end up with 6–8 headings, so use those with the highest scores as your evaluation criteria. Some may have a higher weighting than others so someone needs to do the maths to get the total to 100 per cent.
- Finally, put together the end result of the discussions and check that everyone is happy with where you have got to.

This technique will provide you with an evaluation framework and some potential questions to ask. You will have some idea about whether written responses or scored presentations and scenario workshops are the best modalities for different criteria. You may also have the start of some model answers if you are planning to use those to help with the marking. Further, your prospective evaluation panel will have a shared understanding of what good looks like from a number of perspectives. You will have modelled the alliance way of working and embedded co-production in your evaluation.

Sample evaluation criteria

Tables 3.1a–c present some sample evaluation frameworks. Not all were developed as recommended above and they are here as illustration only, not for you to lift and apply.

Table 3.1a Example 1

Service implementation and operational delivery	Provision of detailed implementation plan	10%	30%
	Provision of detailed delivery plan	20%	
Outcomes	Individual outcomes	9%	
	Style of delivery	3%	
	Demand reduction	9%	30%
	Cost savings	4.5%	
	Social capital	4.5%	
Presentation and interview stage	Innovation, collaboration and promotion of positive risk-taking (for service users) and risk-sharing	20%	20%
Costings			20%

Table 3.1b Example 2

Your alliance group and governance	15%
Service delivery and implementation plan	20%
Collaboration	15%
Performance management	10%
Communication and engagement	15%
Financial framework	15%
Costs	10%

Table 3.1c Example 3

Delivery plans	Transformational change	65%
	Service user need	
	Issues and risk	
	Stakeholders	
	Demand	
	Stigma	
	Implementation plan	
	Management plan	
	Case study	
Finance	Financial plan	30%
	Financial governance and 'Following the Public Pound' code of guidance	
Fair working practices		5%

In Example 3, collaboration and innovation were also tested, but at a different stage.

Provider considerations in alliance procurement

We now turn our attention to the experience of bidders (providers) in any procurement. It may seem obvious to want to be involved in a new collaborative and innovative endeavour as you will be working with like-minded people and, hopefully, contributing to making a big difference to people's lives. However with that opportunity comes responsibility, so it is worth checking that you really want and are able to take this on.

At first glance, being part of an alliance is a no-brainer. Most alliance contracts are for 7–10 years, so there is stability and the guarantee of at least some of the total funding. You will be part of the decision making process for an area of activity that you and your organisation are passionate about. Of course you want to be part of that.

However, your commitment to the alliance and its way of working also needs consideration. Firstly, there is a time commitment, mainly for a small number of leaders but also others in your organisation. This may be problematic for smaller organisations or ones where there are recent or impending changes. Secondly, it is best to be clear about what you are offering the alliance. It may seem obvious to you, but take time to describe this to yourself and to others.

Then there is no guarantee that your individual funding will remain the same. You, along with all the alliance members, will collectively be deciding how to utilise the funds available. Over time there should be shifts and changes that are made according to the 'best for people' principle (see Chapter 2). If the alliance is successful in prevention, early intervention or peer-led support, then, conceivably, service providers may have a reduced role, especially those who have worked in crisis and specialist areas.

Alliances depend on collaborative working. There may be staff members from one organisation who report to another on a day-to-day basis. Decisions that used to be made by your organisation regarding resources, policy and procedures will now need to be discussed collectively and agreed collaboratively. Are you and all those in your organisation ready for that?

Although there are many advantages to being an alliance member, it is not for everyone. It is therefore better to be honest about that from the start than discover it is not for you later on.

Alliance member or network member?

For some organisations, it might be better to remain part of the landscape but not be involved in an alliance. All alliances operate within a wider network of support and services. Some of these may become subcontractors to the alliance. Several of the alliances we have set up work hard to create a sense of inclusivity, with dialogue and events to involve the wider network. An organisation might not be part of the alliance but could still be part of that network.

We used Table 3.2 with one alliance development to differentiate between an alliance member and a network member to help people decide whether they wanted to be considered for the alliance.

Below are a few questions for you and your colleagues in your organisation to help determine whether you want to proceed with bidding to be an alliance member.

Are you right for the alliance?

- What do you bring – expertise, people, resources, contacts, etc. – and are these elements what this alliance needs?
- Have you the capacity to be part of it?
- Will your board or equivalent agree to delegate authority to make decisions to those working in the alliance?

Is the alliance right for you?

- Do the aims of the alliance align with the strategic aims and objectives of your organisation?
- If the alliance is very successful, what does that mean for your organisation? Consider the positive and the negative.
- Will your workforce be happy to be part of the alliance, contributing and working across organisational boundaries?
- Are you ready to move from unilateral decision making on your activities to a collective and collaborative approach?
- If you weren't part of the alliance, would you be able to continue to contribute in other ways?

Table 3.2 Differences between alliance and network members

Alliance Member	Network Member
• Joint accountability for delivering overall outcomes • Shared responsibility for service delivery • Joint development of operating and financial plans • Shared risk for financial performance • Commitment to alliance principles • No fixed individual scope of work or remuneration	• Accountable for delivery of scope of work within their contract • Set commercial and financial arrangements • Adherence to Alliance values and behaviours • Meet standards for Alliance services as determined by the Alliance • Input into whole system service design

Your decision about whether you want to be part of the alliance will depend on many things. Take time to think through the implications from a number of perspectives. Bidding to be in an alliance and then being a member of one is time consuming and intensive. Make sure it is the right decision for you.

Choosing partners

Commissioners will ask for group bids. Those in the successful group will become the provider members of the alliance, joining the commissioners to form the full set of members. The organisations that form each bidding group will have collectively decided that they are the right mix. They then need to persuade the commissioners that they are the best group, both as individual organisations and collectively.

Many provider organisations will be used to joint bids. You may have applied for partnership, consortium or other collaborative tenders. Bidding to join an alliance is similar in many ways, albeit the successful bidders will be part of a more intense collaboration than most are used to.

As mentioned earlier, alliance contracts are usually for 7–10 years, so it is not just about who it is convenient to put together a bid with; it is about the long term and who you want to be alongside for up to a decade. You may want to undertake a more formal due diligence exercise to be assured, and to assure others, that all parties have the necessary capabilities and sustainability.

It is important to be sure that you want to work with others in the group and that they want to work with you. Don't choose partners who will simply help you win the bid; choose them because you want to work with them and deliver together in the long term. And remember there is no 'lead' contractor to orchestrate everything. You are all equals.

Spend time getting to know each other

You may have known other organisations and key people for years. After all, you share the same patch and may have met many times at forums and events locally. You are likely to have a head start with knowing who you would like to be in partnership with. You may be looking forward to working collaboratively with them rather than, at times, in competition.

This is a strong place to be, but it is only the start. Being alliance members together requires strong relationships and high levels of trust. It means taking your entire organisation with you, from the Board to those working everyday with those you serve. It means getting to know the other people and organisations too, finding out about their motivations, personnel and the way they work. We suggest you find time to get to know each other well. Some alliances have arranged day visits to each other's premises, meeting each other's staff. This is time well spent.

As well as getting to know more about each other generally, we recommend you spend some time describing what each organisation brings to the table and what each one wants to get from it. From this, you can explore your alignment with the alliance and each other more fully. You will talk about value creation in two senses: as value creation for your organisation; and how coming together with others will create new value.

Alignment

Alignment with a common goal is essential for all collaborations. To be successful, you need alignment of all parties. Essentially, success for the alliance means success for each member. This sounds obvious, but it needs checking out in detail before and during the collaboration. An active and committed member of an alliance will know that the time and effort involved brings benefits to their own organisation; it will create value for them. The value may be financial, reputational, influence, skills and knowledge acquisition or any other aspect.

In the corporate world, alliances are usually business-to-business ones. Value creation from forming an alliance is a commercial advantage and often linked to building critical mass globally or in specific markets, learning quickly about unfamiliar markets and accessing skills in other geographical locations.

In public sector alliance contracts, we tend to focus on social value. It's not hard to align success for the alliance in how it impacts people with success for organisations that are already trying to do that. But the truth is we also want our organisation to be financially secure. We are just less willing to talk about this.

To explore value creation for organisations, I encourage people to think selfishly. I joke that it is the last time they will be asked to think only about themselves and what they want to get out of this. This usually does the trick. I've even had people say they want to be made an Officer of the Order of the British Empire (OBE) or receive a higher salary. Good, I say – let's be open about that, put it on the table.

More typical responses are about stability and sustainability, funding, growing reach, sharing resources –such as training, back office staff or co-ordinators. There is often something about sharing skills through working alongside people in multidisciplinary teams or having more influence on input to policy locally, regionally or nationally.

The first important thing is to be clear about your own motivations. The second is to be open with potential partners in your bid about what you want to get and what they want to get from being part of the alliance. It is good to have an opportunity to discuss these, to quiz each other and get underneath the high-level statements.

The conversations with potential partners can sometimes be difficult. You are sizing each other up; you are deciding whether to join them in a long-term relationship. The nature of public sector alliances means that providers often know each other well, both as organisations and as individuals. There will be history and shared experiences, good and bad. The first consideration is often whether you have a shared ethos and either similar cultures or complementary ones. If that feels right, the next step is to explore your perspectives in more detail. Spending time at the outset to hear about the expectations of others and to share your own will help prevent misunderstandings and surprises further down the line.

Workshop exercise – alignment

This exercise works well with several people from each organisation.

- Start individually or in organisation groups. Imagine a future where the alliance is successful. What would that look and feel like, what would that mean?
- Now do the same for your own organisation. What would does success mean for your organisation? Jot down your thoughts on a piece of paper.
- Once everyone has had a few minutes to write down their personal thoughts, get together in a group with people from one or two other organisations and talk about what you each have put down. Are there similarities? Are there differences? Is there anything that might be a potential misalignment?
- Note down the key points and, when you are done, feedback the key points from your group and listen to that from others.
- In particular, if there are any obvious or potential misalignments, discuss as a group how these can be reduced, mitigated or removed.

This alignment workshop exercise gets people talking about critical issues. It's important not to take for granted that everyone has the same view of success as you. In one case, we devoted time to this at a two-day away-day during the formation of the alliance. It transpired that one organisation was expecting the alliance to help its ambition to grow, and another was expecting the alliance to help it downsize. This was a surprise and led to a good discussion.

I think it is a great example of a reason to share ideas. Both of these organisations might easily have assumed that the other had the same goal. By exploring how they thought the alliance would help them on their opposing paths, they were able to set expectations and understand what mattered to each other.

Value creation

An alliance is greater than the sum of its parts. Having looked at the value the alliance will create for each member organisation, we now turn to value creation for the alliance itself, what each member brings and how they complement each other.

An alliance is like a team in a race. It is not a loose coalition coming together every so often to see how each party is doing. It is a unified group in the same race and all with a role to play. Each member will bring different and complementary skills to make the team the best.

This sports team analogy comes from *Alliance Advantage: The Art of Creating Value through Partnering* by Doz and Hamel (1998). I was lucky enough to attend Yves Doz's course at INSEAD ('The Business School for the World') in Paris in 2008. Although the book is (and the course was) about business-to-business alliances, many of the concepts, ideas and evidence they discuss pertain to all forms of risk-sharing alliances. Value creation is a major theme in the book – how it is being better to work as a team than individually, and how to build the right team. Doz and Hamel talk about the preconditions for 'racing as a team', such as:

- a strong shared commitment to playing as a team
- the ability to keep one's bearings in unstable conditions and uncharted territory
- a compelling but realistic motive for running that particular race
- wanting to win a race even with different reasons for running in it
- understanding the value of running as a team
- understanding what each member contributes to increase the odds of winning.

As with alignment, the more you can talk openly and honestly about value creation with potential partners in your alliance, the more likely you will be able to understand each other and confirm that you have the right partners. Conversations about insights and shared ambitions will help develop trust and build strong relationships.

Coming together to create value

Innovation depends on different perspectives. Using the sports team analogy, you don't want a football team with only defenders, a gymnastics team where everyone is best at floor exercises or a car racing team with a lot of mechanics but no drivers. This sounds obvious, but it's a reminder that alliances are as much about innovation as about collaboration.

I have been asked about creating an alliance with, for instance, a group of GP practices. Yes, there will be efficiencies from working together, but the opportunity for new thinking might be limited. Pooling ideas and insights, being open to different perspectives, that is where the innovation starts.

I would go as far as to say that you need organisations of different sizes as it is not just about the subject and experience expertise. Small organisations tend to be able to move faster to make changes, while large ones can bring people in to alliance roles short term with less impact on the rest of the business. Small and large organisations also have different approaches to finance and reporting. Neither is right or wrong, so you can bring them together and take the best from each. Ideally, therefore, your bidding group, and subsequently your alliance, will have a mix of organisation types, a mix of sizes and a mix of capabilities.

Pooling resources

Accepting that diversity is important, the next step is to work out the best mix for the context. Here we need to consider what each potential partner brings to the table, such as the following elements:

- people – workforce
- assets – capital, physical, materials
- systems – business systems, technology
- knowledge – technical know-how, community intelligence, customer understanding
- skills and learning
- contacts and networks – brand, reputation, influential relationships
- funds – cash flow, grants
- access – to market, technology.

There will be some overlap of course, but it is fine for one or more organisations to have similar workforce roles for example. The main thing is to have some significant differences and for each member organisation to bring something unique or special. You may decide that, although a number of organisations could bring some specific capability, the alliance will only draw on it from one of them. There are no hard and fast rules. The key is to discuss matters openly and agree together.

Workshop exercise – value creation

This is a good follow-up to the previous exercise on alignment, with several people from each of the organisation in the room.

- Firstly, arrange the participants into organisational groups. Using the list of resource types, ask the groups to write down what their organisation brings to the mix and what they hope others will do.
- Next put two groups together to compare notes. Have they written down similar or different things? Are there any gaps?
- Finally, put more groups together or move to a whole-room discussion. From this you can develop a 'value creation' profile for the potential group of alliance members.

Revisit regularly

As with alignment, circumstances change over time, so make a point of revisiting value creation regularly, actively thinking about what each member is contributing and whether expectations are being met. It is fine to adapt as time goes by, especially if good progress is being made on achieving the outcomes and you want to push yourselves further.

The group bid

Throughout the procurement process you need to show you are the best group: you have the right mix of organisations and people; you bring the right capacity and capabilities; you have great ideas for the future and how to make things better; and you work well together. The easiest way to show you are the best group is to be the best group.

There are many factors that make up a successful bid, and each situation is different. Having been part of or witnessed numerous procurements, two things stand out for me – understanding the requirements, and time and planning.

Understanding the requirements

I will break this down to understanding the client, alliances in general and this alliance specifically.

THE CLIENT

I have been surprised occasionally at the level of disdain some providers have shown for the commissioner, and vice versa. That is not a good starting place for an alliance as the commissioner will be a member alongside the providers. Indeed, the commissioner is the only definite member at the start of procurement; others are being invited as prospective members.

I know there is often a sense that providers know more about the issues than a commissioner sitting in a council or government department. The flipside of this is that the person sitting in the local authority or government department knows a lot more about the whole picture and local politics.

To be successful in the bid, it is worth understanding the (client) commissioner's world view. Don't dismiss it; it is real and based on experiences and perspectives. Get underneath it. What are they looking for? What matters to them? How can you help? How can you demonstrate value for money?

ALLIANCING

The commissioners have chosen alliancing for a reason, and it is likely to be about driving innovation, collaboration, best for people decision making and reducing duplication. You will understand these and other elements of an alliance way of working. It will help if those around you do too, so make sure that key people have had the opportunity to learn about alliancing for themselves.

THIS ALLIANCE

The last element in understanding requirements concerns the specifics of the alliance you are bidding for, especially its objectives and outcomes. You need to commit to delivering these and demonstrate you have delivered them. If you frame as much as possible from this perspective you will be well on the way to showing you understand them and are the best group of organisations to achieve them.

We sometimes see bids from incumbent providers which are, in effect, a continuation of existing arrangements: each provider carries on doing what they are doing now, getting the same 'slice of the funding pie'. This makes no sense. It shows a lack of appreciation of what it has taken for a commissioning manager to push through changes in their own team, department and/or organisation often over many months, even years. It shows a lack of understanding of why the commissioner has chosen a particular methodology to drive innovation as well as collaboration. It also gives the impression that the providers are mostly interested in preserving their own organisations' position rather than what could be done better for the people the alliance is for.

To be the best group you need to clearly and robustly demonstrate that you understand the challenges but also the possibilities; that you are ready for change and excited and eager to be part of an exciting future.

TIME AND PLANNING

Many of us know what it is like to lead a group bid or to contribute to one. There is often a lot of last-minute reviewing of written responses or preparing together on the train journey for an interview.

An alliance bid takes this to a whole different level. You need to convince people that you understand the collaborative nature of alliances, the shared responsibilities for everything, the shared risks. You want people to choose you to be alliance members for 5, 7 or 10 years. It's a long-term commitment. This will require good planning and plenty of time together. For example, one of our alliances held weekly three-hour meetings for many months during the pre-procurement and procurement stages. This meant the bid development was genuinely shared; everyone formed, stormed and normed, and got to know each other well. Their cohesion and togetherness then came across strongly in face-to-face sessions during the procurement and, not surprisingly, they were the successful group. Their time together was well spent; it was an investment that paid off.

In addition, if the procurement process has been designed well, the process will allow you to develop plans for delivery, finance, personnel and other areas so that you can then move easily into the mobilisation phase and put these into action. Again, time well spent. If possible, identify the key people in each organisation who will have roles in the alliance, an Alliance Management Team for instance. They can help with bid development so they must be fully up to speed and ready to go should the bid be successful.

We advise commissioners to build in face-to-face sessions to test collaboration and innovation during the procurement process, such as dialogue sessions, presentations or scenario workshops. Each will differ as to how and what they are scoring, but the focus will be on the group overall.

Of course, you can rehearse so that you come across well on the day, but this step is far easier if you are truly a collaborative and innovative group, working as equals, sharing ideas but not afraid to challenge or bring different views from others. It is very easy to tell a good group from one that hasn't really understood what an alliance means in practice.

Final tips

Group bids can be very time consuming, so it is best to use the time wisely – for the sake of group development as much as for the short-term aim of winning the bid.

- Make sure each member of the group brings something that strengthens the group.
- Select partners for long-term delivery, not to 'win'.
- Understand the client's world view and what matters to them.

- Make sure you and others in your organisation understand alliancing and the alliance way of working.
- Refer often to the objectives and outcomes; place them front and centre of your thinking as well as your writing.
- Plan enough time to prepare written responses.
- Don't 'window dress' team dynamics just before face-to-face sessions; be genuine.
- Keep your organisation updated so there are no surprise challenges at the last minute.
- Involve others in your organisation so that you are ready for mobilisation if you win the bid.

After procurement

Mobilisation

Once the preferred bidder is announced, you can start mobilising. There is much to do in a short space of time as the formal launch of the alliance may be only a couple of months away. We've learnt it is critical to establish the alliance way of working from the outset in setting up the new governance, management and operational structures.

The period preceding the launch of an alliance is a time of intense activity and change as you move from an old way of working to a new one. If there has been a competitive process, you are moving from roles as judges and judged to equal partners sitting around the table. Even if you have not been through a competitive process, it suddenly starts to feel real, and all those things you have been talking about for many months now need to get done. There are all the practical issues that go with any new enterprise: recruitment, information technology (IT) systems, branding and communications, policies and procedures. It can feel like an endless list.

Inevitably, it will feel a little chaotic and not everything will go smoothly. In this section we outline some of the elements you should consider and what we have learnt from experience to date.

No more 'them and us'

Once the procurement process is over, you are now one team. The alliance will be run by providers and commissioners together, and everyone is invested in its success. You all want it to achieve its aims and purpose. You all have that common goal.

Of course, commissioners are invested in the success of all those they contract with or give grants to. However, the culture of competition and contract management has often trumped relationships and collaboration, leading to a default mindset in both commissioners and providers that is hard to move away from. In my experience, it takes time and positive action to move away from 'them and us'. Commissioners will say 'The providers must do x or y', while the providers say 'The commissioners need to . . .'.

Of course, everyone will always have their unique role and perspective; that is what makes alliances so rich. But the shift to collective responsibility, collaborative decision making and no blame, no fault will need a shift in everyone's mindset. This is most easily demonstrated (or not) in the language we use. I encourage people to catch themselves or others if they fall into 'them and us' language. This raises awareness of the new way of working and makes people think about why they still pigeonhole each other into expected behaviours.

Get new governance up and working as soon as possible

Although the alliance is not yet live, we strongly recommend that you set up 'shadow arrangements' that mimic the ones you will have in the future. A Shadow Alliance Leadership Team to govern the mobilisation phase will help get everyone round the table, and you can start putting the Alliance Principles into practice.

In reality, this often means little more than the commissioner representatives of the Alliance Leadership Team joining providers. The latter will probably have been meeting together for months as they progressed through the bidding process. They may already have planned meetings for the mobilisation phase. On one level you can simply change these meetings from provider ones to Shadow Alliance Leadership Team ones by including the commissioner's representatives. The Shadow Alliance Leadership Team will govern the mobilisation and implementation of the alliance.

More importantly though, this marks a move from 'them and us' and 'provider and commissioner' to 'we'. From here on, everyone is working together, making decisions together and acting as one. Up to this point, delivery plans, communications, workforce and any other plans were devised by providers as they prepared by their bids. Commissioners then responded to them, giving feedback in competitive dialogue or negotiations, or a score in a final tender. Now they are jointly owned, refined and signed off.

Separate the final negotiations on the Alliance Agreement

There is one remaining activity to complete that is not for the Alliance Leadership Team: finalisation and signing of the legal deed – the Alliance Agreement. The Alliance Agreement is set by the Commissioners as Owners; it is their document. The other signatories are the alliance providers. In other sectors these are known as non-owner participants (NOPs), which is a pretty stark differentiation. However, an Alliance Agreement is a relational, mutual document focused on common purpose and fair, balanced working arrangements.

We advise that discussions between all parties to finalise the Alliance Agreement are held separately from Alliance/Shadow Alliance Leadership Team meetings as this is not a responsibility or task of those teams. Their meetings should be absolutely focused on getting the alliance up and running, identifying key roles and setting up the management and operational structures to achieve the objectives and outcomes.

Members of the Alliance Leadership Team are often the same people who would be present to negotiate and finalise the Alliance Agreement. The time commitment is heavy for senior people in provider organisations, so it seems obvious to use the Alliance Leadership Team meetings to discuss the Alliance Agreement. Also, there is a new spirit of collaboration, so using a collaborative forum to do this seems appropriate. However doing this would mean the commissioner representatives in the room have to oscillate between being collaborative colleagues and Commissioner as Owner. Depending on whether there are any final sticking points, this can be fine or it can be uncomfortable and delay the transition to future relationships.

We find the best compromise is to hold an additional session after the close of an Alliance Leadership Team meeting to discuss the Alliance Agreement. Commissioner personnel who are not on the Alliance Leadership Team can then join the meeting, and those not involved in negotiations (such as the Alliance Manager), can leave.

Identify an Alliance Manager as soon as possible

In order to progress, you need to identify someone who can work full time and pull everything together. We recommend an Interim Alliance Manager because a full appointment will take time and will need a fully constituted Alliance Leadership Team in place. Also, the skill set in the early months is more like a project manager, someone able to crunch through all the issues and activities at pace. Longer term, an Alliance Manager or Director needs to shift the focus more onto relationships and being able to work strategically and diplomatically between organisations. Either way, you cannot mobilise with just a series of meetings between relatively senior people and an expectation that everyone will be able to move things forward between meetings. That never works.

Changes to alliance members

So far we have focused on members of a new alliance during its set-up. We will now look at changes in alliance member organisations once it is up and running.

Members leaving

When setting up an alliance there is every expectation that the member organisations at the start will remain the same throughout the lifetime of the contract. But things change, so there needs to be some flexibility to the membership of the alliance.

One of the features of alliance contracts is that there is no provision for leaving voluntarily. That is, an organisation cannot say it will sign up at the beginning, see how things go and then decide whether or not to leave the alliance. All parties must be fully committed for the duration of the contract. However, we are now seeing longer contracts as confidence in the model grows, with recent alliances set up for up to ten years. In that timespan, it is not unreasonable to assume that changes within organisations may impact on their role, capacity or commitment to an alliance.

There are two main ways to leave – by mutual agreement or via the wilful default mechanism. The first may be because the member is no longer a main contributor to the alliance or wants to stand down for other reasons. The second is because the member is not behaving in a fitting or appropriate way and the other members wish them to leave.

Mutual agreement

We now have experience of members leaving by mutual consent. The timing and financial considerations will need to be worked through and will be specific to the circumstances, as in this example from the Future Pathways Alliance.

Alliance in practice – Future Pathways

As the initial five-year contract period came to an end, one member of this alliance indicated that they wanted to discontinue their involvement. With the passage of time, there was a need to re-evaluate the alignment between the aims of Future Pathways and organisational direction. Ultimately, this led the member to withdraw as contract renewal was being negotiated with the commissioner.

It helped that the member was open about their intentions, so this development was not a surprise. Offering remaining members a notice period of months was important to ensure the smooth transfer of work and associated information. Of the remaining three members, only two were in a position to take up the work, and one was able to do so. Affected staff were offered roles with a continuing alliance member, thus minimising disruption. Additional work was required to make sure that any information pertaining to the Alliance's work was transferred to a continuing member, in line with data retention requirements in the context of continued service provision.

As the change in membership coincided with the financial year and contract cycles, and another alliance member was able to absorb the work, operational and financial disruption was very limited. Through their role on the Alliance Leadership Team, the commissioner was fully involved and regularly updated about how the departure was being managed, including time frames, financial implications and actions taken to address or limit risk.

The main points from the Future Pathways example are:

- Be clear about the reason for leaving.
- Be proactive in managing and communicating about the exit.
- Plan and record the financial implications.

Wilful default

Wilful default is one of three circumstances in which a member can be removed from an alliance. The other two are insolvency and regulatory failure, both of which would lead to automatic exclusion.

Wilful default refers to repeated non-adherence to the principles of alliance working and good faith. It is thankfully rare, and has not yet happened in any of our alliances. However, on one occasion where a member organisation was causing difficulties, the decision was taken to terminate the alliance altogether rather than try to maintain it with the remaining members. The following is the relevant legal text from our Alliance Agreement template.

Wilful default

In this Agreement the phrase '**Wilful Default**' means that an Alliance Participant has committed one of the following acts or omissions. The Alliance Participant committing the act is called the '**Defaulting Participant**'. The acts or omissions are:

1. an intentional or reckless act or omission by the Defaulting Participant or any of its officers or representatives appointed to the Alliance

Leadership Team or Alliance Management Team which that Defaulting Participant or any of its officers or representatives appointed to the Alliance Leadership Team or Management Team knew or ought reasonably to have known:

   a. was likely to have harmful consequences for the Alliance, one or more other Participants, or the Service Users; or
   b. was a breach of an Alliance Principle or the Alliance Values and Behaviours;

2. an intentional or reckless act or omission by the Defaulting Participant or any of its officers or representatives appointed to the Alliance Leadership Team or Alliance Management Team without regard to the possible harmful consequences arising out of the act or omission;

3. an intentional failure by the Defaulting Participant or any of its officers or representatives appointed to the Alliance Leadership Team or Alliance Management Team to act in good faith as required under this Agreement;

4. a repudiation of this Agreement by the Defaulting Participant;

5. a failure by the Defaulting Participant to honour an indemnity provided under this Agreement;

6. a failure by the Defaulting Participant to pay moneys due under this Agreement within 14 Business Days of being directed to do so in writing by the Alliance Leadership Team;

7. a fraudulent act or omission by the Defaulting Participant or any of its officers or representatives appointed to the Alliance Leadership Team or Alliance Management Team;

8. an intentional failure of, or refusal by, the Defaulting Participant, to effect and maintain an appropriate insurance policy or indemnity arrangement which it is obliged to effect and maintain this Agreement or at law; or

9. an intentional or reckless breach of a confidentiality obligation, or other obligation, in Clauses relating to confidentiality in this Agreement although this does not mean any innocent or negligent act, omission or mistake the Defaulting Participant or any of its officers, employees or agents acting in good faith.

If any of these circumstances arise, there is rectification process to follow. Should change not occur following this, the Alliance Leadership Team can recommend to the commissioner(s) that they formally exclude the defaulting participant. Obviously there will be consequences following the exclusion. Further clauses in the Alliance Agreement describe the principles for handling impacts on finances, transfer of services and survivorship. For example, the alliance may decide to continue with the remaining members or may to invite a new member. This will be highly dependent on the specific circumstances. These decisions are for the Alliance Leadership Team in liaison with the Commissioner as Owner.

New members joining

As with a member leaving, the original members of an alliance at set-up are not expected to change. In practice, however, we have had new organisations join alliances, usually to replace outgoing members.

In any group, new members have to find their place and be accepted by others. The group dynamics will change and take a while to settle. This is no different in an alliance. The existing members will need to get used to new faces, and the incoming member will need to get up to speed with the story to date for the alliance and its ways of working.

Welcoming new members

A new member invited to join will be bringing specific value to the alliance. The invitation will be a shared one by all the existing alliance members, meaning the new member is very welcome. Even if there have already been discussions about the alliance in the build-up to a new member joining, it is worth considering a formal induction package for its Boards, senior executives, key personnel and the wider workforce. This could include:

- general information on alliancing
- the story of the alliance and its Charter – vision, purpose, objectives, outcomes, principles
- information on all the partner organisations and key personnel
- the alliance way of working and how it works in practice
- the Services Operations Manual.

The induction can be tailored to three groups in the new organisation:

- those who will sit at the Alliance Leadership Team – representative and deputy

- those working 'in the alliance', on its activities
- the Board, executives and managers who need to know about the alliance even if they are not actively involved.

There may be others depending on the alliance, such as the wider workforce, both paid and unpaid. The important thing is to not assume people know or will pick things up. A planned set of activities that show you are thinking of everyone will be much appreciated. Similarly, it is important to inform existing members of the alliance and the workforce about the new member, for example through information packs, induction events and other introductory meetings.

Being a new member

It is an exciting prospect joining an alliance, and there is a lot to learn. You and others in your organisation will want to take time to get to know people, their individual and collective history in the development of the alliance and how they work now.

It can be daunting and at times challenging to join a group that has a lot of shared history and established ways of working. Navigating your role in fitting in while bringing new perspectives and thinking that might challenge what has gone before can be a delicate art.

Summary

Its members are the heart of an alliance. Their commitment, their willingness to work in the alliance way, and the skills, resources and ideas they bring will all add to the success of the alliance.

It is not always easy to be part of an alliance, but it can bring great satisfaction. Choosing alliance members or choosing to be an alliance member requires careful thought and many considerations. Procuring members for your alliance is the start of your new way of working. The change in how you act as a commissioner has begun. The way you go about your procurement is a chance to demonstrate that. You are choosing people and organisations who you will be working closely with for several years. This is not a technical exercise; it is about people and relationships.

Everything you do – from the process you choose, to the style and quality of your written material, to the inclusion of the voices and perspectives of people who use your services – will set the scene for how you intend to work in the future.

In the next chapter we will look in more detail at the Alliance Agreement, the formal and legal foundation of your alliance.

References

Doz, Y., & Hamel, G. (1998). *Alliance advantage: The art of creating value through partnering*. Harvard Business School Press.

Veitch, J., & Bland, J. (2023) *Vitalising purpose: The power of social enterprise difference in public services*. E3M. https://e3m.org.uk/vitalising-purpose-book/.

Villeneuve-Smith, F., & Blake, J. (2016). *The art of the possible in public procurement*. E3M. https://e3m.org.uk/the-art-of-the-possible-in-public-procurement/.

Case study 4

Lambeth Living Well Network Alliance (2018–present)

This alliance has responsibility for the majority of adult mental health support and services in Lambeth, including prevention, early intervention and support, as well as many clinical and inpatient services.

The Living Well Network incorporated and built on a previous alliance, the Integrated Personalised Support Alliance (IPSA), for those with severe and enduring mental illness and the Living Well Network Hub and related services. These had been running for about two years, and had already helped reduce the number of referrals to secondary care services while increasing the number of people who were given support.

The Living Well Network Alliance has the same members as IPSA. Alongside the council and its Clinical Commissioning Group (CCG) as commissioners, there are four providers: a mental health trust, adult social care and two charities. The Alliance went live in July 2018 on a seven-year contract with an option for a further three years. Annual funding started at around £55 million, increasing over the first five years to over £80 million.

Creating the Alliance

Lambeth Council and CCG had a positive experience of alliancing with IPSA, which was up and running and doing well by 2016. Lambeth's mental health commissioner, Denis O'Rourke, was keen to start working through how alliancing could be applied to other mental health services.

The main issues in the design of the alliance strategy were the financial elements and the impacts on local providers, especially the mental health trust. This meant a lot of preparation work and discussions with senior leaders to ensure people felt the proposed alliance was beneficial for them. In addition, NHS England commenced its Independent Support and Assurance Process for complex contracts, so we needed to ensure we kept it updated and informed and took on board its feedback.

Lambeth Council and CCG issued an open Expression of Interest Notice to test market interest in the proposition. As only one credible application was received, they considered there was no viable market and proceeded to direct negotiation with that group, which comprised existing members of IPSA with good experience of alliancing. Negotiations moved to a shared task of developing a robust delivery and financial plan for the first two years of the contract. This took several months and much revision as funding allocations and ambitions for change needed to be reconciled.

Shadow governance was set up in autumn 2017 and, together, the alliance members took responsibility for developing the plans. The appointment of the Alliance Director was pivotal as he brought leadership to the developing alliance; and, along with colleagues from all the member organisations, was able to inject pace and detail into the various plans and policies.

A specific feature of the Living Well Network Alliance is its range of subcontractors, which include organisations in housing, employment services and other sectors. Understandably, they were keen to know how decisions about commissioning their services would work in the future. The members of the alliance spent time considering how they would collectively make decisions, the criteria against how decisions would be made and the associated risks.

Progress of the Alliance

The new alliance went live in July 2018 and continues to this day. Early successes include the opening of a number of Living Well Hubs around the borough. They developed their own 'Alliance Way', namely: to keep support and services person-centred; to focus on people's strengths rather than their weaknesses; and to be compassionate and respectful, while continuing to remain relevant and provide value for money.

The Covid-19 pandemic naturally had a major impact, with changes to how people worked during lockdown restrictions and increased demand for mental health services.

This alliance is notable for its stability and leadership. There have been a few changes in key people but enough continuity of roles to maintain stability. Importantly, the same person has held the Commissioner as Owner role throughout, despite NHS reorganisations that could otherwise have derailed the Alliance. There is a strong focus on values, relationships and good governance, which has allowed changes to be made over time and has seen the Alliance through difficult times and crises.

Aisling Duffy, Chief Executive of Certitude, one of the Alliance member organisations, also stresses the importance of governance maturity. Even after six years, they talk about checking and reviewing governance as the Alliance shifts over time. As the Living Well Network Alliance is a large one covering many teams and services, there is active investment in team development. This allows for greater delegation and leaving people to get on and do things, always informed by the Alliance Way.

What changed for people

Lambeth's Living Well Alliance has six priorities that build on the original three big outcomes of the Living Well Collaborative:

- Reduce numbers of people reaching crisis point, and give prompt and appropriate support for people in crisis.
- Increase numbers of people able to live independently.
- Increase numbers of people living in stable and appropriate accommodation.
- Improve mental health outcomes for members of the black community in Lambeth.
- Improve physical health for people with mental health issues.
- Increase numbers of people in education, training, volunteering or employment.

All plans and reports are based on these priorities giving a clear focus for all the Alliance does. The published annual reports provide rich information on the Alliance's impact on both numbers and narratives.

Reports are available at https://www.lambethtogether.net/living-well-network-alliance/reports/.

4 Alliance agreement

When setting up an alliance, it is important to focus on what you are trying to achieve and the relationships you need to make that happen. Only once these are clarified and in place should you turn your attention to the legal document you need to underpin your collaboration.

The Alliance Agreement is the legal contract that describes your way of working as a group of member organisations and individuals in the alliance. It signals and supports your desire to work in collaboration with others.

In this chapter we look at the differences between an Alliance Agreement and a usual service contract. We work through the typical content and common questions, noting what is usually settled at the procurement stage and what is finalised subsequently. There is also an explanation of how financial and commercial arrangements have been developed in other sectors. At the end of this chapter you will have a good sense of the elements of the Alliance Agreements we have used and the rationale behind them.

I am not a lawyer, so the content here is from the perspective of a lay person who has had the privilege of working alongside lawyers as we developed alliances. You will have your own legal advisers to give specific guidance.

A relational contract

Any contract is, in principle, a mutual agreement for mutual interest, and this applies especially to an Alliance Agreement. The key difference between an Alliance Agreement and a usual service contract is that the Alliance Agreement is a risk-sharing contract, not a risk-allocation one. It is a relational contract.

Alliancing is a form of outcome-based commissioning, where the vision and outcomes you expect the alliance to achieve are agreed from the outset but the way in which alliance members agree to deliver and co-ordinate the activities to achieve them will change over time. The legal agreement reflects this. It is not a contract for specified services. There are clear, practical and proportionate descriptions of the objectives and collaborative way of working, with a positive focus on public value and effectiveness rather than a negative one on protections and remedies for contractual failure.

DOI: 10.4324/9781003511809-4

One of the things that first struck me when I started working with lawyers who had developed the Alliance Agreements in other sectors was that the documents were relatively short and straightforward, especially given they were the legal basis for high-value (often multimillion-dollar) contracts.

The main content differences in an Alliance Agreement are:

- The language uses 'We' and 'Us' rather than, for example, 'The Company' and 'The Provider'.
- It starts with the vision, purpose, objectives and outcomes.
- There is no rigid and prescriptive service specification.
- It describes the commitments, governance and decision making.

An Alliance Agreement does, however, contain a lot that you are used to seeing in service contracts, such as clauses on liability, termination, disputes, intellectual property, invoicing and reporting.

It can sometimes be hard to persuade colleagues to let go of their service contracts. These are often standardised for local councils and other public sector commissioners, and have been carefully thought through by legal and procurement personnel. Moving to a new and, for them, untested contracting method feels high risk. Unfortunately, attempts to 'fudge' the move can occur, and there are so-called 'Alliance Agreements' in circulation that demonstrate this.

Fudge 1 – Service contract with an alliance schedule

We have experience of a so-called Alliance Agreement being nothing more than a typical service contract containing a schedule on alliancing at the end. While this allowed the alliance to be created and was accepted as a compromise by those in place at the time, it meant that anyone joining later who wanted to understand the new approach was confused on reading the contract. There were internal inconsistences, and the style and wording did not match expectations of the spirit or working of the alliance.

This halfway house approach demonstrates a lack of support for the move to a relational, risk- and responsibility-sharing way of working on the part of the legal advisers.

Please avoid using this approach. The alliance using it managed as there was a strong collaborative spirit in place anyway, but there were times when the disconnect was problematic.

Fudge 2 – Service contracts with an 'overlay' Alliance Agreement

In other sectors some alliances have linked service contracts in certain situations where there are specific reasons. We prefer to avoid this as there is no need because your Alliance Agreement should cover all matters.

However, alliances that are underpinned by individual service contracts form the model adopted in NHS England, as reflected in its template Alliance Agreement. If you were to search online for 'Alliance Agreement' you would soon find the 2016 NHS England Standard Alliance Agreement, which refers throughout to 'NHS Service Contracts'. At that time there was a statutory requirement in NHS England to use the NHS Standard Contract for all health-care services other than primary care. This meant you couldn't just have an Alliance Agreement. It had to refer to and be underpinned by NHS Service Contracts between each provider member and the commissioners. This, in effect, made the NHS Alliance Agreement template an 'overlay agreement' to service contracts. Indeed, in order of precedence, the service contracts come first.

This model is also not something we recommend. While not without some merit, it is a different type of collaboration to the risk- and responsibility-sharing of a whole system inherent in the alliance model and defined in our Alliance Agreements.

The main practical impact of this watering down is that any collaborative, unanimous, best for people decisions made by the alliance that mean a shift in service delivery, and therefore financial flow between alliance members, will then need to be reflected in variations to the relevant service contracts. Not only does this add an extra series of steps, but it also risks the changes being blocked or delayed in one-to-one negotiations. In essence, it leaves you with all the same issues of traditional service contracts.

I will not go into more detail here. Much of the NHS version looks and feels like our template as the NHS one is built on our material and our legal adviser's input. Suffice to say that, if your alliance is led by an NHS England Health Commissioner or has significant input from an NHS England organisa-tion, you may have to use NHS England Standard Contracts.

We were in this situation with our Lambeth alliances, so we used a worka-round and, importantly, kept the Alliance Agreement at the top of the order of precedence. We used the phrase 'refer to the Alliance Agreement' throughout the individual NHS Service Contracts to avoid describing activity and remuneration in each. This workaround, coupled with highly committed alliance members, allowed the spirit of true alliancing to exist alongside the statutory requirements.

On the upside, two legal firms cross-checked the two volumes of NHS Terms and Conditions with our Alliance Agreement, so we were confident there were no inconsistencies. On the downside, whereas most of our alliances have just one legal agreement for everything, the Lambeth Alliance has six.

Fudge 3 – Alliance Agreement mandating competition between provider members

Another unhelpful variation in one alliance was an added schedule that described situations in which the provider members had to compete with each other. It was designed to be only for any new monies added to the alliance funding, despite that not being deemed necessary in any other alliance. As it turned out, there was some over-interpretation by provider members competing to decide who did what within the alliance. This went as far as the members planning subcontracts with each other. An unhealthy obsession with competition and contractual arrangements developed, which led to strained relationships and too much energy and time spent on this rather than on the core purpose of the alliance.

In other alliances, when there are planned service changes or new funds become available, the Alliance Leadership Team can use a range of ways to allocate funding. Sometimes they choose to use a competitive process, with written bids and interested parties recusing themselves from decision making. In other situations they make the decisions against set criteria, but without the formality of a competitive process.

The important point is that they have a choice; and, whatever approach they decide to take, they can justify it on the grounds of probity and good governance.

Template Alliance Agreement

In 2013–2014, working with international law firm Gowling WLG on our first alliances, we developed an Alliance Agreement template. Although the main clauses are relevant to any alliance – including governance and roles, and performance and finance – the schedules are bespoke for each alliance, and we give suggestions for the content of these.

We wanted to move away from the formalised, legalistic, conventional, commercial drafting that is often believed to be unavoidable. We tried to make the language as free from jargon and impenetrable legalese as possible. This wasn't easy and the result is not perfect, but we feel it is an improvement on previous versions.

The template Alliance Agreement has been used by most of the alliances we have set up. We have made minor changes over time based on experience and feedback.

Main clauses

The main body of the Alliance Agreement is divided into four sections.

Section A

This sets out the vision, purpose, objectives and principles of the alliance. In essence it is the Alliance Charter. Apart from the 'values' and 'behaviours' clauses, you should be able to populate this in full in draft stage.

Some people will find the language you use for this section a bit woolly for a legal document. Interestingly, we had this tested in one of our alliances. When we moved from the first Lambeth Alliance to the second, larger one, there was a new director in one of the provider organisations. A meeting was held to discuss the Alliance Agreement, which is based on the one we used for the first alliance. The new director questioned the first section and suggested we remove references to 'vision' and 'values' as, in his words, they were not relevant in a legal document. However the response from all those who had worked as part of an alliance for some time was a resounding and collective 'No'. For them, framing and setting the context for the alliance and its way of working were importantly reflected at the beginning of the legal document.

Section B

This sets out the roles in and the governance of the alliance, and includes clauses on the commissioner's two roles, and those of the Alliance Leadership Team (ALT), the Alliance Management Team (AMT) and the Alliance Manager. Decision making and any decisions that remain for the commissioner only are also covered. Other clauses cover disputes, transparency and ethical walls. We look at roles and governance in detail in Chapter 5.

Section C

The third section mainly concerns the principles behind performance, financial risk and benefit-sharing mechanisms, with detail given in separate schedules.

Section D

The last section details the remaining contractual terms, including intellectual property rights, confidentiality, termination, liability and indemnity. Your legal representatives will be able to advise on these, so we won't go through all of them here. However, there are two questions that come up frequently that I will expand on a little. As mentioned earlier, I am not a lawyer. My comments are therefore based on experience and knowledge of alliance ways of working and the information I have picked up by working alongside lawyers as we have developed alliances.

LIABILITY AND INDEMNITY

The principle of collective responsibility often raises questions about liability as people are understandably concerned about being held to account for the actions or omissions of other members. They might worry about regulatory action or the financial implications of something they feel is not within their control. It is always helpful to explore the kinds of examples they have in mind and work through these together. We usually find there are sensible and practical solutions for various scenarios.

It is usually obvious where an act or omission was clearly attributable to an individual organisation or to multiple parties, for instance mixed teams or personnel from one organisation in the premises of another. The latter situations are not unique to alliances; they are already happening, so issues such as liability are already being addressed. An alliance is no different.

EXIT OF ALLIANCE MEMBERS

Another common question concerns what happens when one or more alliance member is not performing well. People ask about the contingencies other members have to address this; or someone may ask about leaving the alliance if they no longer want to be a member.

We covered this situation in the previous chapter, with the main point being that there is no provision for leaving an alliance voluntarily as all members are expected to fully commit for the duration of the Alliance Agreement. However, as noted in Chapter 3, we have experience of members leaving by mutual consent, with arrangements made by the alliance and the Commissioner as Owner.

Schedules

The schedules in an Alliance Agreement are mostly specific to each alliance. We'll run through each, highlighting the content you will need to decide.

Schedule 1 – Definitions and interpretations

This is pretty set, but there may be a few superfluous terms or terms that need amending for your context.

Schedule 2 – Scope of services

Describing scope can be tricky as you need to provide enough information without falling into the trap of describing current services. That could give the impression that you expect things to stay as they are, or not change very much. We also advise against dropping in the delivery plan from the successful bidders as this is the opening delivery plan only and would be expected to evolve over time.

Much of the text can be taken from the prospectus you created for the procurement process (see Chapter 3). Start with the basics about the people the alliance is for:

- who – adults, children and young people, people over a certain age
- where – residents of your town/borough/city/county; there is often a nuance here if the NHS is involved as it could include all those residing in or registered with a GP in the area
- the specific group (if relevant) – for example, those living with dementia and their families and carers, people experiencing mental distress, people with severe and enduring mental illness, people who are homeless or at risk of homelessness.

Then move on to the expected types of support and services, always accompanied by wording such as 'including but not limited to'. Try to keep the language generic and avoid using named current services if possible.

OUT OF SCOPE

It is often helpful to describe what is beyond the scope of the alliance. To avoid a long list, concentrate on those areas closely linked to its activity.

Successful alliances quickly gain a reputation as problem solvers. Not surprisingly, they are then asked to solve problems outside their initial remit. While some may be easy to accommodate, the additional work may start to impact on finances and capacity. Where there is a chance that new responsibilities might be added over the lifetime of the contract, at the outset, you can explain this and the process for agreeing on expanding scope. Some alliances have successfully expanded their scope and been given extra resources to do so. This helps everyone as no one wants the alliance to end up taking on more than it can achieve within the funding available.

SERVICES OPERATIONS MANUAL

It is useful to understand how you agree the service delivery model and activities when working as an alliance. The absence of a service specification in the contract does not mean there is a free for all.

A lot of detail is needed to describe activity and delivery, but these are not fixed for the duration of the contract. The way support and services are delivered and arranged should look very different at the end of the contract life compared with the beginning. For instance, there will be technological advances, new ways of working, efficiencies and sharing of back office and workforce development. Alliancing is a methodology for change and

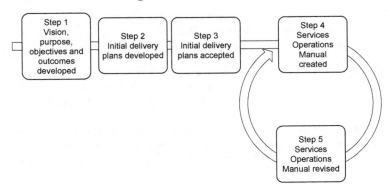

Figure 4.1 Services Operations Manual development process

innovation, not just collaboration. This is why you don't need service contracts to 'underpin' the Alliance Agreement or a long list of delivery detail in
the Alliance Agreement itself.

What you do need is clarity among alliance members about who is doing
what. This is the idea behind the Services Operations Manual, which is owned
by the alliance and constantly reviewed and updated. Some alliances use the
term 'Operating Framework' or similar but, for simplicity, I'll use Services
Operations Manual throughout.

Fig 4.1 shows the usual sequence for deciding on delivery in an alliance
and developing the Services Operations Manual.

- Step 1 – The Alliance Agreement sets out the vision, purpose, objectives and outcomes, based on all the inputs and insights from those who
  have contributed. The overall scope and any service standards are also
  described.
- Step 2 – As part of the commissioning process, the prospective alliance
  members submit detailed, costed delivery plans for how they would meet
  the objectives and achieve the outcomes, in the first year at least. The plans
  will describe the responsibilities of each organisation and their expected
  funding.
- Step 3 – The Commissioner as Owner decides which bidding group best
  meets the evaluation criteria, including the robustness and feasibility of
  delivery and associated financial plans.
- Step 4 – Once the alliance is formed, the delivery plan is implemented.
  An Operational Framework or Services Operations Manual is then created, which describes the alliance's business processes, policies and procedures. This is owned by the Alliance Management Team and updated when
  needed. It is a useful resource for existing and new personnel.

- Step 5 – As needed or at regular intervals (at least annually), the delivery and financial plans are refreshed, unanimously agreed and then implemented. In this way, changes to services are made over time and reflected in changes to the financial plan. Changes might come from new learning, external environment changes or success in, for example, reducing crisis and therefore more investment in prevention.

All changes are described in the Services Operations Manual, so there is no need for changes to legal documents or for separate service contracts.

Schedule 3 – Performance framework

Performance reporting will be based on the set of outcomes you have co-produced, – the things that, from different perspectives, matter to people. As part of the bidding process, bidding groups may have been asked to explain how they intend to demonstrate the alliance is achieving its outcomes. They will create the performance detail and processes, usually through negotiation so that, together, you agree a version that will be used as the alliance commences.

At draft Alliance Agreement stage, you can have a placeholder for each outcome and await details when they are agreed later. You will need to describe the expected timings of any reports and any other particulars that are relevant to you. For instance, there may be mandatory reporting that the alliance will need to provide for national data collections.

GAINSHARE AND PAINSHARE

These are key aspects of alliance contracts used in other sectors and form part of their performance framework schedules. In adopting alliance contracting in the UK public sector, we have found that gainshare and painshare are not widely used. This may reflect the introduction of alliance contracting in the UK at the same time as austerity and much-reduced funding for public services. If overall funding is very tight, there is no room for gainshare payments. Holding back certain amounts of funding to then be 'given' for high performance levels is, as most providers would be very quick to point out, a form of inverse painshare, not gainshare.

Where we have used gainshare and painshare, in the first Lambeth Alliance, they became important areas of focus even though the amounts of money involved were relatively small. These aspects were felt important enough to keep in the second Lambeth Alliance, albeit only from the third year. As it happened, this coincided with the Covid-19 pandemic, so, amid all the other pressures and new demands, they were understandably not implemented.

Schedule 4 – Financial framework

This will cover issues concerning commissioner to provider and provider to provider. It could also include commissioner-to-commissioner financial and risk-sharing arrangements, although, to date, we have tended to keep these in a separate agreement. This is pragmatic as any alliance forms part of wider collaborative arrangements between local authorities and NHS commissioners, so is covered by an existing agreement under Section 75 of the National Health Services Act 2006. Most of the items in the financial framework will be set out by the commissioner, although there will be details to finalise once the alliance provider members are known.

FUNDING

Details of funding allocations usually include:

- a table of allocation for years 1 and 2 with indications for the remainder of the contract term
- expected reductions or increases year on year (if any)
- the process for confirming each year, dates and how the alliance will be notified.

Although you are unlikely to be able to confirm funding over the lifetime of the contract, you should be able to give some indication of the direction of travel. In some alliances there has been a set year-on-year reduction in overall budgets. In all cases, it is wise to include the caveat that year-on-year changes will be reviewed in light of the local and fiscal environment at the time. It is also important to establish and set out the process and timing for when the alliance will have its funding allocation confirmed each year.

COSTS

We recommend including the following:

- a list of the type (not the amounts) of core costs (pay and non-pay costs) that are eligible as alliance activity
- a list of costs that would not be considered alliance ones
- levels of overheads for each provider
- gainshare and painshare (if relevant), split between providers, and the process for their determination over an agreed time period.

Clarity about permitted costs highlights what can and cannot be included in the financial plans, both at the outset and in years to come. You may want to include a catch-all term about 'any costs unanimously agreed by the Alliance

Leadership Team as relating to alliance activity', or perhaps list the headings for inclusion – for example, salaries, training related to alliance activity, administration and co-ordination, legal fees, etc. It is important to also list any that should be excluded. In the end, most of our alliances take a pragmatic and flexible approach.

Overheads are usually estimated by adding a percentage to all pay costs or to the overall budget agreed for an alliance provider member. Levels do not have to be the same for each member; indeed, there may be good reasons for different levels. The only rule is that everything is openly negotiated (i.e. no one-to-one side conversations) and unanimously agreed.

INVOICING AND PAYMENT

This part of the performance framework schedule will include the usual details surrounding invoices and payment terms, namely:

- frequency – whether each provider invoices against a plan or via a 'host banker'
- the reconciliation process between providers for variations and movements against a plan.

There are two common arrangements for invoicing and later reconciliation. In the first, each alliance provider member invoices the commissioner or lead commissioner for a set amount based on the agreed financial plan. Whether this is monthly, quarterly, in advance or in arrears will be dictated by the commissioner's usual financial arrangements.

The second arrangement involves a host banker. Here, one of the alliance provider members invoices the commissioner or lead commissioner for the total amount at the agreed intervals and then passes any funds due to other alliance provider members. It is important to stress that this is a technical role only and does not mean the provider raising the invoice is a lead provider. All financial decisions regarding alliance activity and remuneration are made by the Alliance Leadership Team and then enacted by the host banker.

In both approaches, a reconciliation process is needed if activity changes during the year and there is an increase or shortfall of actual costs against the plan. This is usually done at least annually.

COST AND ACTIVITY REPORTING

The expected reports to the Commissioner as Owner from the Alliance Leadership Team will need to be described here, as well as any process within the alliance for collating financial reports and approving them collectively.

AUDIT AND RECORDS

Any stipulations about keeping records and audit requirements will need to be added here if not already in the main clauses of the Alliance Agreement.

Schedule 5 – Governance roles

We use this schedule to list the named representatives and deputies for the Alliance Leadership Team and Alliance Management Team at the start of the contract.

Schedule 6 – Service standards and requirements

This schedule will list any relevant requirements that are in the commissioner's usual service contracts.

Other schedules can be added as required, for instance, data-sharing protocols.

Finances, risk and change

We have talked about the Alliance Agreement and the reasoning behind some of its content. Here I want to emphasise a few points about alliancing in general and how these impact on the way collective risk and finances are handled in an alliance.

Shared finances

A major distinction between alliances and most other collaborations is the shared risk and responsibility for the overall finances. This is the game changer. It requires new conversations, new thinking and openness. Shared responsibility makes it harder for people to continue protecting expensive and risk-averse practices when they can see the impact this has on other parts of the system.

A colleague who has worked in alliances in other sectors once told me that the only way to truly change behaviours is through financial incentives. I was highly sceptical of this. As a health professional working in the public sector all my life, I believe that there are other, more important, motivations. Yet I was already aware that how money flows through a system and financial norms and regulations create certain behaviours. That is why I became interested in new commissioning and contracting models in the first place.

Different funding arrangements for GPs, social care provision and hospitals means there are all sorts of anomalies: people seen in hospital accident and emergency (A&E) departments and not outpatients as remuneration differed; GPs asked to prescribe medication on the instruction of a hospital because it comes from a different budget; the community team who say 'We can't do that because we are not funded for it.' Never mind the inconvenience – money flows dictate or are used as an excuse for behaviours.

Was my colleague correct? Will change only come if there are financial incentives to change? Of course, change can come in many different ways, for example from necessity, spending time together or shared learning. For me, it is about creating an environment in which change can happen, and this includes changing how money flows around the system, who makes the decisions and how financial decisions are made. While not the only ways, these can be very powerful catalysts for creating new thinking and new ideas.

Alliances allow you to make those changes. Instead of having a public sector funder who dictates who does what and for how much, alliances have a shared funding pot and shared decisions. Lucy Dadge, Director of Integration at Nottingham and Nottinghamshire Integrated Care Board, was one of the instigators of the Mid Notts Better Together Alliance. She makes the point that a truly pooled budget is essential for sharing financial and delivery risks. While the Better Together Alliance was groundbreaking as an integrated strategic alliance in England, it had a very wide in scope and multiple members. It was only when it created a smaller, more focused alliance in the form of the End of Life Care Together Alliance that they were able to have a pooled budget for a specific pathway for a specific group of people (see Case Study 5).

The only certainty is that things will change

Being an alliance member is often seen as a way to secure funding for an organisation for the duration of a contract as the typical term for Alliance Agreements (5, 7 or even 10 years) is highly favourable compared with the one- or two-year contracts that went before.

However, to be truly innovative, alliances need to be able to move resources around. A common reason to create an alliance is to increase preventative work and reduce the need for more expensive specialist and crisis activities. It is obvious therefore that the alliance member that undertake those higher-cost activities will need to adapt.

This goes back to our earlier discussion on alignment and misalignment. At the outset, you must set the expectation of change. You need to be able to move money around the system, to allow funds to 'follow the person'. Therefore, on signing up to an alliance, every member organisation needs to consider how it might flex and adapt its activities. Everyone needs to accept that their share of the funding may go down over time.

This sounds positive and, in the main, it is. However, collective decision making about money is not easy. As someone from one of our early alliances said, 'We all get on fine until we talk about money.'

Risk exposure

In any alliance there will be organisations for whom the alliance is a small part of their business and others where it is all or a very large part. This is healthy in that you get a mix of perspectives, but it can also lead to tension, especially around differences in risk exposure.

Most alliances work on the basis that any sharing of finances, for instance to fund central costs or cover overspends, are calculated as a proportion of the overall budget that each provider member receives. For example, if alliance Member A receives 10 per cent of the overall budget, it will contribute 10 per cent to costs, while member B receiving 30 per cent will contribute 30 per cent.

This is simple and straightforward. However, it might hide the fact that the 10 per cent of the overall funding that Member A receives represents 90–100 per cent of its total turnover. In that case, any additional costs or pressures have a very different impact to Member B, who receives 30 per cent of the alliance funding – but this represents less than 5 per cent of this organisation's total turnover. If you add in the position on reserves – where, for the sake of this example, let's say Member A has very few reserves but Member B has comfortably large ones – you can see how their risk exposures are very different.

Lack of transparency or understanding of these differences makes it even more difficult to talk about money. As always, the advice is to be open and not shy away from the difficult conversations. In one example, the alliance allocated a simple equal share of the budget and risk among all provider members. However, this had a disproportionate impact on the smaller members. After a number of years, the Alliance Leadership Team collectively took the decision to alter the financial arrangements to acknowledge this impact and make things fairer for all.

Commercial frameworks in other sectors

Public sector alliances in the UK tend to keep financial and commercial elements relatively simple. However other sectors take a more detailed approach to commercial aspects when creating alliances and setting up their commercial frameworks. The aims and principles are to drive innovation and collaboration while being fair and equitable to all. Linking everything to achievement of the aims and outcomes of the alliance helps avoid perverse incentives.

Here I discuss some of the concepts as there are important principles at play, even if your own circumstances mean you cannot take full advantage of the benefits they bring. I am indebted to Andrew Hutchinson of Alchimie Pty for much of the information in the remainder of this chapter.

Definitions

When we adapted alliance contracting for the UK public sector, one of the things we had to do was change some of the language. For example, we removed the words 'commercial' and 'profit' as these do not play well in public, charitable or voluntary sector discussions, and we tend to replace 'commercial' with 'financial'. Yet there are important differences between meanings that we should not ignore:

- The word 'commercial', as an adjective, means 'concerned with or engaged in commerce' and 'making or intended to make a profit'.
- The word 'financial' means 'relating to finance' – in this case, the finances or financial situation of an organisation or individual.

These aspects both concern money, but commercial is also about trading, business and enterprise. While we would not say our primary aim in wanting to join an alliance is to drive profitability, we should not be naïve in thinking that commercial arrangements do not matter in public sector alliances.

Even though statutory and charitable alliance members don't have shareholders to think about, people will want their own organisations to be viable and to be able to pay themselves, their workforce and their bills. We all want our future to be secure and are invested in the financial aspects of our organisations. Each organisation needs a sound, sustainable financial base and reasonable surplus for its development. Therefore, a profit margin should be included in project costs, albeit for different reasons and scale to the commercial concept of profit maximisation as a principle driver.

Although we have tended to minimise the importance of the commercial aspects of alliances in the UK public sector, it is worth understanding how commercial aspects can be intrinsic parts of alliances and, far from hindering collaboration and innovation, can actually drive them.

Commercial framework ethos

In an alliance, the commercial arrangements underpin the collaborative way of working. The premise is that everyone wants everyone to succeed and no one wants anyone to go out of business. We are all in this together and want to achieve the goals and outcomes together. If any one party fails, then all will fail. Put simply, we all win together or lose together.

Commercial framework principles

It is important to establish a set of principles that guide the design of the commercial framework. Overarching principles might include:

- There will be cost transparency between providers (subject to compliance with competition law and the need to ensure non-disclosure of commercially sensitive information).
- Value for money must be demonstrated in all alliance activities.
- No one party shall derive unreasonable advantage or suffer unreasonable disadvantage.

Commercial framework structure

The basis of the commercial framework is to align the commercial interests of the provider members with the owner's set of outcomes and objectives. Provider members need to have an equitable (not necessarily equal) share in the value of achievement of the alliance outcomes. This is structured around the key result areas (KRAs) of value to the owner, and therefore to the people the owner represents. Fig 4.2 describes the overall commercial framework.

Actual costs

The left-hand side in Fig 4.2 represents the reimbursements based on scope of work – that is, the actual costs related to activities undertaken by each provider in the alliance. This core remuneration package covers all alliance-related expenditure plus an agreed corporate overhead and marginprofit.

Direct costs

Direct costs are any costs or expenses incurred by the alliance members in performing work under the Alliance Agreement, such as for staffing, materials, rent, legal advice and so on. Proposed principles relating to direct costs might state that:

- We cannot recover anything that is not a bona fide specific cost or expense incurred by us in performing the work under our Alliance Agreement.
- We can only recover a maximum of 100 per cent of any bona fide specific cost or expense incurred by us in performing the work under our Alliance Agreement.

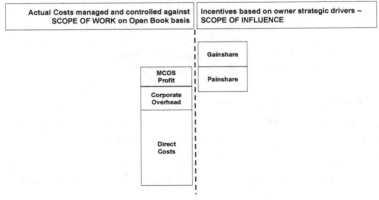

MCOS = Minimum Conditions of Satisfaction

Figure 4.2 Alliance commercial framework overview

Reimbursement of actual costs – as opposed to funding to the target costs/ target outturn costs (TOC) or budget – is a mechanism to drive efficiency. It means that providers are not encouraged to 'spend to their budget', and instead should be looking to control costs and, where possible, make further savings. The desired outcome is a reduction in actual costs against target costs. This should not be a reason to artificially inflate target costs. Transparency about target costs, including contingencies, is essential.

The reimbursable direct costs need to be agreed in advance. Providers will usually submit target costs and how these are derived during the bidding or mobilisation period. The target (outturn) costs are primarily an agreed scope (in terms of performance), an agreed method of costing that scope, and agreed contingencies and risk factors on the costs. All parties want and need a *right* cost.

The extent to which the owner scrutinises these is for them to decide. One approach is to undertake an independent audit. The advantage here is that there is corroboration of how each provider has derived its costs estimates, which will increase provider-to-provider as well as owner-to-provider trust. The independent auditor can also be asked to comment on any areas of commercial sensitivity where pricing should not be shared between providers. In these instances a mechanism to share information with the owner but not the other providers would need to be created.

The list of reimbursable costs will be included in the commercial framework schedule in the Alliance Agreement. The direct costs should include salary and on-costs (additional costs to employers to hire staff, such as pension contributions) but not corporate overheads.

Corporate overheads

Predetermined corporate overheads can be agreed for each provider, and can differ for different providers. For example, in one of our alliances one provider was getting 17 per cent, another 10 per cent, another 7 per cent and the fourth zero. This reflected one taking on the role of host banker and associated transactional costs, as well as the different sizes of the organisations.

As an aside, it is not uncommon to hear commissioners talk about not wanting to fund anything other than project costs for charities and not-for-profit organisations. It seems to me that this represents a lack of understanding about how any business, whatever its make-up, is run. Even the leanest organisation will need to dedicate some of its workforce time to keeping the organisation ticking over. There are insurance and accountancy fees and subscriptions for IT and other services. Corporate overheads must therefore be factored in.

Minimum conditions of satisfaction profit

Any profit for member organisations will only be paid if performance exceeds the minimum conditions of satisfaction (MCOS); and, as we discuss below, that profit can be at risk or enhanced depending on performance. Arriving at the terms for MCOS and profit levels is challenging as the principle is that the alliance members have been chosen for their ability to deliver outstanding performance. Therefore, reaching minimum expected performance levels should be seen as disappointing. The opportunity to achieve significant margins or profits should only be possible with gamebreaking performance.

Incentives – gainshare and painshare

The right-hand side of Fig 4.2 shows the overlying gainshare/painshare, which is linked to performance in a few key areas. Here, it is the influence a provider has on the performance rather than its relative cost that matters – hence the label 'scope of influence'.

GAINSHARE

The gainshare is an agreed amount based on performance over and above the MCOS, up to game breaking achievement. The gainshare regime is a performance-based incentive paid to or by the alliance members. It will be for actual performance of work under the Alliance Agreement in order to share the gain and pain, in pre-agreed ratios, of actual achievement. It is intended to reward, and therefore drive, outstanding performance.

PAINSHARE

The painshare is a subtraction of the core package when performance falls below the MCOS. This can impact margin/profit and, in cases of very poor performance, some or all corporate overheads.

Gainshare and painshare are designed to drive changes in behaviour and performance and provide opportunities for gamebreaking achievements. The design needs to be specific for each alliance as its members, aims and outcomes will differ.

With any incentive regime there is the risk of creating perverse incentives and unintended consequences. To minimise this, it is best to keep it simple, have underpinning principles and involve everyone in the design. Below are examples of gainshare/painshare principles used in other sectors:

- Gainshare/painshare provides the only performance-related payment mechanism.
- Cumulative provider painshare is capped at a level unanimously agreed for each party.
- Commissioners are committed to the providers earning 100 per cent of their possible gainshare entitlements.

- The only way to exceptional return is gamebreaking performance.
- Each provider has a meaningful incentive to exceed minimum performance.
- It should be clear, concise and easy to understand and apply but not easy to deliver gamebreaking performance objectives.
- There is complete transparency in all gainshare arrangements.
- The separate elements of the gainshare regime are interdependent to provide no incentive to sacrifice performance in one key result area to secure reward in another.
- The only acceptable outcomes are win/win or lose/lose; there should be no opportunity for win/lose.

PERFORMANCE THRESHOLDS

The gainshare regime is built around a spectrum of performance comprising levels of performance ranging from failure, through MCOS (or business as usual) to gamebreaking (or outstanding). Performance thresholds and associated measurement methods will describe various levels of performance. The thresholds are not targets. There is no sense of 'You must achieve this or else.' Thresholds describe different points along a spectrum.

The thresholds can be at intervals (shown by the blocks in Fig 4.3) or linear (shown by the continuous line). Numerical measurements (for instance, bed days, numbers of people in settled housing for at least six months) can be

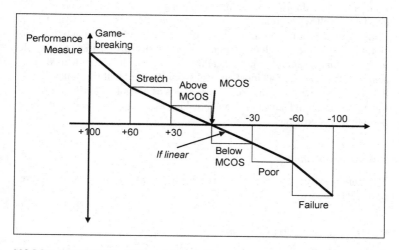

MCOS = Minimum Conditions of Satisfaction

Figure 4.3 Spectrum of performance

anywhere on the line. However, if the level of performance is more a judgement of achievement (moving, say, from good to excellent), then a stepped or block approach would be more suitable.

GAMEBREAKING

The setting of gamebreaking performance is a technique for 'achieving the impossible' in alliance. We are familiar with stretch targets in health and social care – where a stretch threshold means the best level of performance that can be achieved by doing what we do now consistently well.

Gamebreaking, on the other hand, is so ridiculously out of the question that the only way to achieve it is by doing something completely different. Indeed, when the gamebreaking threshold is described, it needs to be beyond anyone's imagination that it could ever be achieved.

How does that translate into practice? Imagine that there are five key result areas and each has 1, 2 and 3 measures. In total there will be 12–15 performance measures and you set a gamebreaking threshold for each of those. Now let's say you have created the alliance well, with all members aligned and committed to change, development and innovation. Putting their heads together and being free to think the unthinkable, they might just be able to achieve gamebreaking performance in, say, one or two, maybe three, of those performance measures.

The alliance has achieved the impossible.

It is this possibility of achieving something that no one thinks is possible that lands well whenever I have spoken about alliances to a new audience. Going back to that first example in the oil industry in the introduction to this volume, they came in well under budget, six months early. These are tangible outcomes that are hard to find in health and care. The first Lambeth Alliance achieved the closure of an inpatient high-security ward within 18 months due to lack of requirement. Had we set thresholds as part of a gainshare regime, I imagine this would have been gamebreaking as we certainly would not have thought it was possible.

Types of performance

There are usually two types of performance linked to gainshare and painshare: cost and non-cost.

COST GAINSHARE AND PAINSHARE

Cost gainshare regimes typically involve a simple sharing mechanism for performance against target costs.

UNDERSPEND AGAINST TARGET

In cases of lower actual costs against targets, a mechanism is needed for how this amount is then shared between the owner and the providers. This must be agreed in advance and stated in the commercial framework schedule of the Alliance Agreement.

BENEFIT SHARE

One approach is to divide any underrun equally (50:50) between owner and providers. The providers will then need to agree a formula for how they will apportion the amount between them.

Commissioners are sometimes concerned that underspend in the alliance will be used by providers to subsidise other parts of their business. We have usually included a provision in the Alliance Agreement schedules that any underspend is used for the benefit of people living in the city, borough or county represented by the commissioners.

An example of a cost performance framework is given in Fig 4.4.

The top left of the graph shows a 50 per cent split of over- and underspend between owner and commercial participants. If there is a large underspend, some of it is allocated to a performance pool.

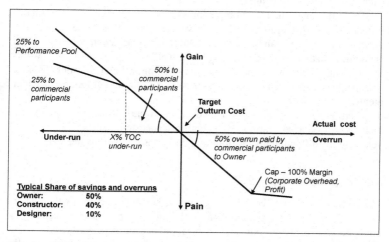

TOC = Target Outturn Costs

Figure 4.4 Sample cost performance framework

PERFORMANCE POOL

A performance pool or 'gainshare pot' means that underspent money is available for use by the alliance as a whole rather than being returned to each provider member. One popular method in the alliances we have set up is to use any underspend for innovation projects or additional workforce training and opportunities. This means the funds continue to be used for the benefit of the alliance.

OVERSPEND

There is a risk that the actual costs may exceed target costs. A similar decision about how this is then borne by the owner and the providers is needed. There may be a willingness to share risk up to a certain degree, after which it becomes a provider-only risk. In the example in Fig 4.4, any overspend or overrun is split 50 per cent between owner and commercial participants. If the overrun (bottom-right corner) becomes very large, there is a cap to prevent the 'pain' impacting direct costs for the latter.

Interestingly, we have found that overspends are discussed differently by those in the statutory sector and those in voluntary and community organisations. The latter operate on a cash-in-bank basis so cannot overspend, whereas the statutory sector is used to going 'above budget'. The discussions about these different approaches are illuminating and allow for some healthy exchanges and shared insights.

Of course, any alliance can have 'pressures on its budget' (to use a statutory sector term). Unfortunately, we have seen this for ourselves, especially during and since the pandemic as demand has increased considerably. There is no question that financial stress will test an alliance and collaborative working. It is easy for commissioners to revert to command and control behaviour and for there to be a deterioration in trust and commitment among provider members.

There are no easy answers. However, good early warning systems and realism, as well as aspiration and a continued focus on goals and values, will help. But the difficult conversations and decisions will still be needed.

Non-cost gainshare and painshare

The non-cost performance will be against the key outcomes set by the owner, who typically provides a lump sum or sliding scale pool as an incentive to innovate and to pursue outstanding performance in these key result areas. Separating the achievement of these from cost performance reduces the likelihood of sacrificing performance in other key result areas in order to reduce cost. A small set of key outcomes is needed, as outlined in the performance framework from a construction sector alliance (Table 4.1).

Table 4.1 Example alliance performance framework outline

Key result area	Minimum conditions of satisfaction	Outstanding performance objectives
Cost	Deliver project within budget	Deliver the project for 20% under budget
Schedule	Deliver the project on time	Deliver the project six months early
Quality	Deliver the project to agreed specifications (workmanship and design)	Deliver the project to agreed benchmarks of outstanding workmanship Design the project to agreed benchmarks of high levels of integration with existing and adjoining assets
Community	The project is not delayed by community or stakeholder opposition to the project	There is widespread community advocacy and support for the project.
Operability	Operators and end users are generally satisfied with the delivered asset	There is widespread support and high levels of satisfaction with the delivered asset

I was interested in how the alliance measured community impact and surprised to find they used a pretty simple questionnaire. A minimum of 100 responses was needed – not a very high number considering the large sums of money that depended on the results.

This performance table was a real eye-opener for me as, in health and social care, we can agonise for ages over a particular outcome, defining the measures, analysing and arguing over their reliability and validity. In other alliances, they took something that was 'good enough'. It may not have been perfect or especially rigorous; but it was enough for them, and large amounts of money were passed on or withheld on that basis.

Fig 4.5 shows the numerical aspects of a sample non-cost performance framework.

There are a few things to note in this example. For example, let's say that it relates to the time to finish a construction project, the point of handover to the client. The central point where the two axes cross is the minimum conditions of satisfaction (MCOS) – that is, the project finished on the expected day.

Now let's say it finishes early. For each day early, you move along the x-axis towards the left and will get a corresponding gainshare shown by the plot line. However, there is a limit at +100 (this is meant to be 100 per cent but, for simplicity, let's say 100 days). When this is achieved, you have hit gamebreaking performance and, in this example, there is no further added gain for going further. Another example may have the line continuing indefinitely, but in this case maybe the owner wanted to recognise great achievement but allocate funds to other performance areas.

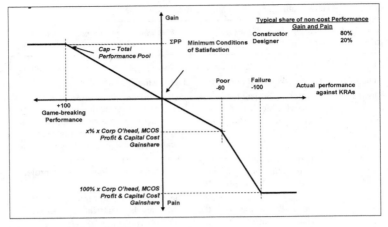

TOC = Minimum Conditions of Satisfaction

Figure 4.5 Sample non-cost performance framework

Fig 4.5 also shows poor and failing performance. The angles of the plot line show that days of overrun will result in a painshare, eating into the agreed profit. This is initially at a similar ratio to the gainshare, but once a certain level of delay has occurred (here at 60 days), the penalty becomes more heavily weighted, as shown by the steeper plot line. Furthermore, you can see that this also represents the point at which the painshare is now affecting corporate overheads. Once the performance becomes so poor that all profit and corporate overheads are removed, there is a floor – the painshare does not increase. This goes back to the principle of not wanting member organisations to be unable to cover their core costs.

This sample graph is just one way to set up the gainshare and painshare for a particular performance measure. There are many other ways, such as only having gainshare with no painshare, or vice versa.

DISTRIBUTION BETWEEN PROVIDER MEMBERS

Once the overall gainshare has been decided for an area of performance, a decision must be made about distributing the gainshare or painshare among provider members. In the examples in Figs 4.4 and 4.5, the boxes show how the distribution was made between owner, designer and constructor.

Each performance measure could have different percentages. Say, for example, one member organisation has the most influence over achieving a particular outcome. In that case, you may want to weight their contribution (both for gain and pain) more highly than for other organisations. Alternatively, you may want to keep things simple, for instance according to the percentage of overall turnover for each member. So, for example, a member who receives 40 per cent of the turnover for the activities and delivery they undertake will take a 40 per cent share of the gain or pain.

There are no rules – just that you follow the principles and use the gainshare and painshare to drive innovation and focus on the objectives and outcomes.

Tracking performance

Performance is assessed at agreed periods (typically bi-monthly or quarterly) to determine the level of performance achieved. There should be an agreed approach about when any payments are made or withheld, whether in advance based on forecast positions or left to reconciliation at the end of each year or total contract life.

Commercial alignment

It can be hard to imagine how to go about getting an openly negotiated, unanimously agreed commercial framework with all the performance thresholds and detailed distributions for each. Fortunately, we have a lot of experience to fall back on. There is a well-established process for this devised by Alchimie Pty in Australia that includes a number of steps. As always, it is important to work through these and carry out each step well to maximise the effectiveness of the next one. The steps to achieving commercial alignment are illustrated in Fig 4.6.

Step 1 – ALT commercial discussion

In project alliances, Alliance Leadership Team commercial discussions would take place as part of the procurement process, in the selection workshops. This step is held with each bidding group and is part of the evaluation of bidders. The purpose of the discussions is to clarify the handling of

ALT= Alliance Leadership Team

Figure 4.6 The commercial alignment process

commercial matters and develop the actual commercial framework. A typical agenda covers the following:

- Alliance Leadership Team and Alliance Management Team – confirm nominations, agree practicalities of meetings (chair, frequency, quorum, etc.)
- workforce and resourcing – approaches to alliance resourcing, employment relations, approach to mobilisation, team-building and coaching
- commercial alignment principles
- critical issues – including interface with key stakeholders, alliance brand, insurances, delegation of authority
- feedback from bidders on Alliance Agreement
- project development phase – determining the process for aligning on target outturn costs.

As you can see, commercial alignment involves much more than just finances. It is not just a financial discussion for financial colleagues. It is also about alignment on governance, key shared issues (such as workforce and branding) and the Alliance Agreement.

Step 2 – Establishment audit

The purpose of the establishment audit is to ensure that all ALT members have enough information to hold an informed conversation about each participant's corporate overheads and MCOS profit. It forms a fundamental part of the probity validation process. The specific objectives of the establishment audit are:

- To substantiate historic records of corporate overhead and MCOS profit margins through scrutiny of company and divisional (as required) financial information.
- To substantiate project management accounts, identifying tendered margins and actual outturn margins on at least ten (typically) recent and relevant projects (both good and bad) of similar nature and size to the current project. The financial auditor may review outturn data of more projects to confirm the appropriateness of the proposed sample.
- To confirm or amend the schedule of direct costs as distinct from corporate overheads. Typical areas of clarification include:

  ◦ rates, salaries, internal costs and their method of calculation (including basis of recovery and utilisation factors, etc.)
  ◦ full-time staff holidays and whether included in direct costs or corporate overheads
  ◦ the application of statutory and other on-costs to payroll

- ° subsidiaries (e.g. plant hire); whether profit centre/cost centre; how the market is tested
- ° overtime and bonuses
- ° for designers, distinguishing between local overheads treated as corporate overheads and those that are part of the cost of providing project resources
- ° differences in corporate overheads for contract versus salaried staff.

- To confirm or amend the commercial framework guidelines, including calculation of direct cost payments and invoices.

The corporate and project figures will be used to substantiate the corporate overhead and MCOS profit margins that will form the basis of Alliance Agreement.

The establishment audit is a key part of due diligence and shows a high level of rigour in considering each member's financial and accounting arrangements. As well as enabling informed discussions about margins, it is also the basis for ensuring that the alliance can produce combined financial reports. There is transparency about how costs are presented in all organisations, which gives everyone confidence.

On the one occasion we undertook a similar audit in our UK public sector alliances: we instead called it a 'convergence audit' and focused on the compatibility of accounting systems for the non-statutory members. A separate, due diligence report was also undertaken to assure the commissioners of the financial stability and sustainability of those members.

Step 3 – Commercial alignment workshops

These are held with the preferred bidding group after the selection workshops in order to agree on the following objectives:

- terms and conditions of Alliance Agreement
- definitions of direct costs
- percentages of corporate overheads and MCOS profit
- gainshare regime structures
- project development phase budgets
- process and key approval requirements for developing TOC and KRA performance benchmarks
- shared understanding of what could constitute a scope variation.

Commercial alignment workshops typically take place over two or three consecutive days. If necessary, they can take up to a week, as was the case with the alliance set up in the aftermath of the earthquake in Christchurch,

New Zealand, in February 2011. Here the total funding for horizontal rebuild (roads, utilities, services, etc.) was NZ$2.8 billion, and the alliance included a number of co-funders and five construction companies. Time was of the essence and they dedicated five days to go through all aspects of the commercial alignment, after which they had reached a consensus and were able to sign the Alliance Agreement there and then.

Two or more full days with senior people and, at times, financial and legal advisers may feel excessive. However, the end point is a fully agreed Alliance Agreement with commercial arrangements, including any gainshare and painshare regimes. Undertaking this bit by bit over weeks or months could take a similar amount of time or even more in the end. In addition, this time together is very valuable for building relationships and achieving common purpose and shared understanding.

Good planning and resourcing of the workshops are essential as there are a lot of topics to cover and many decisions to make. A series of highly structured sessions with facilitators need to be scheduled, and key decision makers should be in attendance throughout.

Step 4 – Commercial finalisation workshops

After the intensity of the commercial alignment workshops, it is sensible to pause while the paperwork is drawn up and any outstanding issues resolved. A commercial finalisation workshop is held about a week after the alignment workshop to review the re-drafted Alliance Agreement, incorporating output from the selection and commercial alignment workshops and for the ALT to finalise all outstanding issues and draft details associated with executing the Alliance Agreement. This workshop closes with the signing of the Alliance Agreement.

Step 5 – Project development phase

Once all of the above tasks are accomplished the governance structure and commercial framework for the alliance will have been established. There are, however, two fundamental items still to be determined: (1) target outturn costs (TOC); and (2) the benchmarks for each Key Performance Indicator (KPI).

- Target outturn costs relate to spend at the end of the project, similar to annual budget setting in public sector financial planning.
- Target costs and performance benchmarks are determined during this final phase by all Alliance members together. This ensures shared ownership and, coming late in the process, means the focus beforehand is on strategic alignment, values and commitment to innovation and collaboration.

Summary

Alliance contracting provides a legal, financial and governance framework for collaborations that are strong, of public value, purpose-driven and risk-sharing. Your Alliance Agreement sets out these aspects and needs to be right for your context. Here we have covered the principles behind Alliance Agreements and how they have been constructed for our alliances in health and social care as well as in other sectors.

In the next chapter we turn our attention to alliance governance and how alliances work in practice.

Case study 5

Mid Notts End of Life Care Together Alliance (November 2018–present)

This alliance was set up for people identified as being in the last 12 months of life. It offers a range of services, from support in the early stages of the end-of-life pathway to the bedded and more intensive support in the latter stages. It comprises two NHS Trusts, two hospices and the local Integrated Care Board (ICB). Its annual budget is £4.3 million and the initial contract was for five years, with a five-year extension now in place.

Creating the Alliance

End of Life Care Together was created as a subsidiary of Mid Notts Better Together, a large strategic alliance in place since 2016. The Mid Notts Clinical Commissioning Group and Nottinghamshire County Council had formed Better Together as a vehicle to focus on integration across all health and care (excluding some specialist services).

A Leadership Team was set up and met regularly. While the overarching alliance did not progress to a legal one with a pooled budget, smaller integration projects were created. One was for end-of-life care, where it was recognised that the multiple layers and people delivering care to people in the last stages of life was confusing and difficult to navigate.

The End of Life Care Alliance partners therefore came together to design a new service model, initially in response to a service specification set by the then Clinical Commissioning Group (CCG). However the group took this further and, through much greater collaboration and partnership, was able to really push boundaries in developing the new model. They used Alliance Principles and 'right care at the right time in the right place', helping a move away from organisational silos to best for service through collaboration and partnership. The new service went live in November 2018.

Lorraine Palmer, the Interim Managing Director of End of Life Care Together, talks about the importance of transparency and openness from the outset. All members coming together early on ensured care was joined up and responsive through a culture of collaboration, partnership and trust.

A cost envelope was identified and, while each provider retained a bi-lateral contract with the CCG, an Alliance Agreement was put in place that described the Alliance's governance arrangements. This meant they could keep individual provider contractual arrangements while setting out new ways of working together, including the seamless moving of resources and the delegated autonomy for decision making within the identified cost envelope.

Progress of the Alliance

The Alliance invested early in local hospice services, delivering care closer to home and in education and training. It aimed to deliver a single pathway underpinned by proactive support and care navigation for patients entering the service. In its first two years patient stories and feedback confirmed the qualitative benefits, and there was a measurable reduction in emergency attendances and non-elective admissions, with significant financial benefits.

The middle part of the initial five-year contract was impacted by the pandemic, but the partners were able to share and move resources in light of ensuing restrictions and infection control issues. This was helped by including the commissioners as a partner, which mitigated the traditional parent/child scenario to a level playing field in terms of influence and decision making. Post-pandemic, the Alliance regrouped and, through the commitment of the existing partners and working collectively with the ICB, was awarded a contract for a further five years in October 2023. This second phase will see the inclusion of three more partners from the hospice and charitable sectors, enabling the Alliance to expand its boundaries in delivering specific components of the model across the county.

The inclusion of continuing healthcare fast track as an integrated part of the pathway, rather than a distinct and separate process, will enable the Alliance to provide personalised and tailored care. This will significantly benefit patients and carers in accessing the service and enable the Alliance to invest in care delivered directly rather than through contractual frameworks. The learning, trust and partnerships built in the first five years will enable the Alliance to develop the new service model and meet its aims of extending beyond the Mid Notts footprint.

What changed for people

From the onset of the service more people were involved in decision making around their wishes and planned place of care. Identification and recognition of end-of-life care needs have increased by 65 per cent since 2018. In working more closely with its members, the Alliance has removed duplication of services, with the aim of easing navigation through services in times of crisis. A key focus was recognising that knowing what was available, how to access it and who to ask helped mitigate distress and crisis at an extremely emotional time and was critical to patient experience. As Lorraine Palmer says:

> End of life care offers one opportunity to get it right but multiple opportunities to get it wrong. Patient stories often told by their carers and relatives have told us we have got it right, but we also recognise there is always areas to improve, something all the Alliance partners are committed to listen and respond to.
>
> The strength of our Alliance is our focus on the needs of the people using our services and continually striving to improve what we offer. That has been one of the greatest strengths of the Alliance and has an unwavering commitment from all the partners involved now and for the future.

5   Alliance governance

People considering using an alliance approach often ask how alliances work in practice. It can be hard to imagine a group of organisations sharing responsibility and coming to unanimous decisions. Who does all the work, how do things get done? In this chapter we explain how alliance leadership and governance are organised and what makes the collaboration work. We look at key roles and how to minimise duplication.

At the end of the chapter you will be familiar with both the overview and detail of alliance governance, including common issues and how to avoid or mitigate them.

Governance and virtual organisations

There are numerous definitions of governance, so people should choose the one that makes most sense to them. I like Good Governance Improvement's reference to 'steering': it's about where you want to go; what course you need to plot to take you there; and how quickly you want to get there while keeping your crew and passengers safe. You need early warning systems you can trust, and professionally trained crew who are clear about their roles and know what to look out for (see https://www.good-governance.org.uk/).

Setting up governance roles and structures is fundamentally about making sure the right people are making those 'steering' decisions, how and where decisions are made, and what the criteria are for making decisions. Decisions are made every day, and the quality and timeliness of decision making reflects whether a governance system is working or not. And, of course, collaborative decision making is all about people and relationships.

Governance also means assurance and accountability. Both are important, and roles, reports and structures need to be built in. So how do you create an environment for collaborative decision making, assurance and accountability that is lean and flexible? Luckily, we have the experience of those who have been setting up alliances for nearly 30 years. As we've adapted their models for the UK public sector, we've made some changes but have kept to the main principles and structures they use – because they work.

DOI: 10.4324/9781003511809-5

A virtual organisation

Although an alliance is not a legal entity, it helps to think of it as a 'virtual organisation': it will need the same roles, structures and processes as any other organisation of equivalent size and range of activities. This helps put things into context. It also allows you to set expectations about timescales. I often hear people in new alliances say that things are moving more slowly than they had hoped. New enterprises often take 1–3 or even more years to really get motoring. Of course, it is good to keep the pressure on; but it is also good to be realistic.

Each alliance is different, and the extent to which you put structures and people in place will depend on the amount and range of activities it undertakes. I find turnover a good guide too. For example, you can ask what you would expect for an organisation with a turnover of, say, £2.5 million a year that runs support systems and services (including a central co-ordination function) for over 3,000 people across a wide geographical area.

As we have learnt, an alliance differs from other start-up businesses in that it is made up of existing organisations. This is a great benefit as there will be experienced people willing to help and specialist resources readily available. It also means that the alliance's infrastructure needs to be lean. You will not want to replicate everything that each organisation is already doing for governance, accountability and management. The alliance sits between and it should complement rather than duplicate. This is the trick, and may take a few iterations to get right. Clarity of roles and the principle of delegation within the alliance governance and management structure will help reduce duplication.

Before we look at governance structures and roles, a recap on alignment is needed. Without alignment, no amount of graphical representations of organisational structure or decision flow charts will lead to good governance or good decision making. I would go as far as saying it is unfair to put anyone into a governance role of an alliance if their own organisation is not aligned with the alliance as a whole or with other parties involved. It puts that person in an impossible situation, and there will be inevitable conflicts.

You need good alignment in order to have good governance in an alliance.

Alignment

If your alliance has been formed through a procurement process, it is likely that the providers in the bidding group will have checked they are aligned with each other: they will have a good mix of capabilities and are all invested in achieving the shared purpose, the common goal. As the alliance forms, commissioning members come together with provider members. You will need to revisit alignment and understand all perspectives in order to avoid any presumptions and misunderstanding.

Different aspects of alignment

There is more than one type of alignment, and here we will focus on the following:

- goals
- drivers
- values
- commitment
- governance.

Goals

Alignment of goals means that the strategic objectives (goals) of each member organisation align with everyone else's, and being a member of the alliance will best help each organisation achieve their own strategic objectives. This should be relatively simple, and sharing each member's strategic objectives helps everyone understand each other and each other's perspective. Similarities and differences between strategic objectives are a good starting point for conversations.

Drivers

I use this to describe more short-term issues. It's best illustrated by thinking about misalignment. For instance, if one of the member organisations finds itself in financial difficulty, its focus will be to turn that around and build financial sustainability. Its ability to be part of a multiparty collaboration may well be constrained during this period. Its immediate drivers are different to those of others.

Another example might be recruitment. In recent years difficulty recruiting has been a constant theme in health and care. Alliance member organisations often need to fill posts not only within the alliance but also in other areas of activity. It is easy to imagine where the drive to fill posts within and without the alliance can be in conflict.

There may be no easy answers to these very real and practical issues, so the key is to be open about them, to keep talking and help each other out where possible.

Values

It can be easy to assume that the kind of organisations that want to sign up for an alliance will have similar values. This is usually the case; but there can also be subtle or not so subtle differences. Comparing values is a great group exercise. It can be part of creating the alliance's own set of values, building on or amalgamating the values of individual member organisation. Through discussion and curiosity about each other's values, you will get to know and understand each other's history and priorities. You can discuss what people actually mean by their words, mindful that organisations may use the same words on the page but mean different things. You can talk about how you would see the values brought alive in practice. In this way any alignment or misalignment can be identified and discussed.

Commitment

Commitment in this context means the willingness to act in the alliance way and adhere to the alliance principles. This can be seen in the way individuals as well as the whole member organisation sign up and behave as alliance members. It means the Board or Trustees are willing to delegate decision making to the alliance; people are prepared and able to attend meetings; and everyone understands and promotes the aims, values and priorities of the alliance.

We find that size of organisation impacts on commitment in different ways. Small organisations may find it harder to commit to meetings if just one or two people have to cover everything. On the other hand, they are the member organisations that often receive the largest percentage of their turnover via the alliance, so are highly committed in other ways.

The opposite is often true for larger organisations in that the alliance might be a small part of their overall business, so the understanding of what an alliance entails may not run deep. Their ability to attend meetings can be constrained when the person nominated also has responsibility for other activities in the organisation.

These are just examples of differences that need acknowledging rather than problems in themselves. As with all the alignment elements, it is important to identify where there is good alignment as well as real or potential misalignment. This is important at the outset but also needs revisiting from time to time. Difficulties arise when they are ignored or result in behaviours that lead to resentment, assumptions and misunderstanding.

Governance

The last element is alignment of the governance of each member organisation. There should be nothing about the governance of the alliance as a whole that does not fit with the governance of each member organisation. The alliance cannot override the constitution of its member organisations.

Where there is a potential misalignment, it is usually straightforward to sort out. For example, one of our alliances has a local branch of Age UK as a member, an organisation aimed at people over 50 years of age. The alliance in question is for all adults so, as a member, Age UK has equal and shared responsibility. A conversation and exchange of correspondence with Age UK's national Board of Trustees was therefore needed to confirm alignment of its constitution and the aims of the alliance.

Checking alignment

Conversations about alignment will be helpful and enlightening, and you might also identify some potential misalignments. This is important as it is critical to reveal these early on even if you are unable to mitigate or remove them. Transparency and understanding are better than ignorance or denial.

Workshop exercise – strategic alignment

This exercise can be done with Alliance Leadership Team (ALT) members, but it can also be useful with others involved in the alliance and key strategic partners. For instance, commissioner organisations often have teams or departments that will end up working closely with the alliance but may not have been involved during the procurement process. Mutual understanding between the alliance and its members is often a key factor in whether or not innovation and improvements can be implemented.

Start individually or in organisational groups, and explain that you are checking everyone is aligned and understands what that means for all. You can also mention that there may be misalignments and that they cannot be ignored. Explain that the session will identify any real, perceived or potential misalignments so that everyone can understand them and plan to mitigate and help each other with them.

Each person or group then spends some time thinking about the alliance using the following questions, either considering them all at once or individually:

- Will being a member of the Alliance help us to achieve our organisation's goals and strategic objectives?
- What are our main drivers at the moment? Does the Alliance help with these? Are any of our drivers going to impact adversely on our membership and commitment to the Alliance?
- Are we committed to working in the alliance way? Are we sure everyone else is equally committed?
- Are there any conflicts between our own constitution and governance and that of the Alliance?

After considering each individually or in a small group, come together as larger groups and discuss similarities and differences.

I've always found that people are very willing to share their perspectives, often coming up with personal and, sometimes surprising, reflections. Honest discussions about alignment and any misalignments will foster trust and build relationships.

Misalignment

In my experience, one of the reasons large-scale change programmes fail is through a lack of acknowledgement that one or more parties will end up worse off if it is successful. Using UK NHS examples, we expect hospitals to take part in initiatives to reduce outpatient appointments or prevent admissions. Yet this is the very reason for hospitals – their *raison d'être*. It is what they are paid for and the basis of their funding. Yes, they may want to reduce excess or inappropriate demand; but, after that, they do not want to close wards, reduce staff numbers or lose training accreditation.

People sign up to high-level aims about improving people's lives, for example. No one would disagree with them; but, as the details unfold, reality kicks in and progress stalls. I would say this is normal. Each of us would do the same thing in their shoes. People feel loyalty to their organisation, their colleagues, their own position and security. Why would they help bring about something that might jeopardise these?

Having said that, I have known people who will make those sacrifices if it means better outcomes for those they serve: the Chief Executive of a homelessness support charity who said his dream was for his organisation to close because it was no longer needed; or the service managers and workforce who have been willing to be redeployed in new roles, seeing the opportunities these bring for themselves and those they serve.

Of course, all change brings benefits and risks. We cannot pretend that change won't mean things will be different and that there will be impacts on member organisations. Hopefully most of the impacts will be positive, but inevitably some may be negative.

Before the collaboration even begins, it is important to put all the potential misalignments 'on the table'. Be honest about them, talk about them, look at how, collectively, they can be reduced and mitigated. In one example, success meant downsizing a clinical department. One of the senior clinicians was due to retire, and the programme was paced so that the change fitted with the timing of the retirement. This meant the organisation was not left with reduced income but with the same fixed costs.

Alliances are usually created to enable change and innovation. With good alignment, the benefits should outweigh the risks for everyone involved. It can be overly simplistic to say you are trying to achieve a win-win situation on every major decision, but having a way to think about how close (or far) you are from that may be helpful. Creating the context where you can consider potentially difficult decisions means openness across all aspects of alignment.

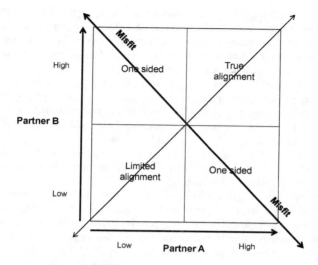

Figure 5.1 Alignment and misalignment

I find the example in Fig 5.1 useful to illustrate the potential for conflict when there is a gap in alignment. It's based on Nielsen's 2010 article on strategic fit and governance in alliances.

Let's take the issue of working in the alliance way – with transparency, no blame, best for people decisions, etc. – and think about how committed to this each partner is. Ideally, you want to be in the top-right box of 'true alignment' – when Partners A and B are both highly committed to the alliance way of working. This will create the best conditions for alliance.

If Partners A and B have low levels of commitment you will be in the bottom-left box – 'limited alignment'. No disparity but not a very promising situation. If one partner is highly committed and the other not, there will be frustration from the highly committed partner and the inability to benefit from the alliance way of working. This is a one-sided relationship and will inevitably lead to failure. You can apply the same dynamics to any area of alignment and commitment.

Alignment between all members of an alliance is a prerequisite for alliance governance. Don't assume it is there because everyone has signed up to the high-level vision. Actively checking and rechecking all aspects of alignment throughout the lifetime of the alliance will help prevent problems building up.

Basics of alliance governance

Alliance contracting is based on shared risk and responsibility, and this is made possible through the joint governance and management structure. The governance arrangements are designed to ensure that decisions are made for the right reasons, and that everyone who is part of the risk share (has 'skin in the game') has a say in those decisions.

If we think of an alliance as a virtual organisation, we can see that it will need similar governance and management structures you would see in an actual organisation of similar size and undertaking similar activities. It will need a 'Board' (the Alliance Leadership Team/ALT), a 'Chief Officer' (the Alliance Manager or Director), and an 'Executive' (the Alliance Management Team/AMT). Fig 5.2 shows a typical governance and management structure for an alliance, with the box formed by the dashed line representing the virtual organisation – the alliance.

To keep the governance structure lean, efficient and effective there needs to be clarity about the roles and responsibilities of each element and minimal duplication of responsibility. This is especially important for the dual role of the commissioners – one as 'owner' and one as 'alliance participant'. It can be hard to imagine how this works in practice. We covered the two distinct roles in Chapter 1, but we will recap here as it is an important issue.

Commissioner as Owner

The Commissioner as Owner role is similar to the role in traditional commissioning. In health and care, the commissioners are acting on behalf of the people

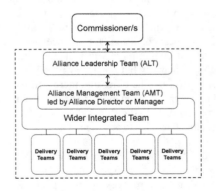

Commissioner as Owner
sets mandate, outcomes, financial allocation, etc for the Alliance

Alliance Leadership Team
senior members (including commissioner) with authority to commit on behalf of their organisation

Alliance Management Team
key people with subject expertise from each of the participating organisations

Alliance Director or Manager
runs the alliance ('go to' person)

Figure 5.2 Alliance governance overview

they serve to identify and fund activities to meet statutory requirements and community benefit. As the 'owner' the commissioner or co-commissioners sets the mandate, the outcomes and the funding envelope for the alliance. They appoint the other alliance members and the alliance is accountable to the Commissioner as Owner throughout its lifetime.

Once in place, the alliance will make all major decisions about activity and utilisation of the funding it has been awarded. There are a few reserved commissioner-only decisions and sign-offs, such as any changes to alliance members; but, other than these, the Commissioner as Owner has no involvement in the running of the alliance.

Regular finance and activity reports to the Commissioner as Owner will provide information on achievement of the alliance's outcomes and value for money. Activities within the alliance, including any undertaken by subcontractors, are all governed and monitored by the Alliance Leadership Team.

Commissioner roles in practice

In order to keep the Commissioner as Owner role separate from the role within the alliance, we recommend that they are held by different people. Usually a more senior person is the Commissioner as Owner (e.g. a Chief Executive or Director of Finance), and a Commissioning Manager or someone with specific subject expertise is the Alliance Leadership Team representative.

In some alliances, the Commissioner as Owner role is held by a group or committee, especially if there is more than one commissioner. This works well as local authorities and the public sector are used to joint committees and other statutory arrangements. Alliance reports are formally submitted to the meetings of the group or committee. There are variations in practice.

For example, while the Commissioner as Owner is a senior person in the County Durham Mental Health and Wellbeing Alliance, a Commissioning Manager embodies the role. She meets regularly with the Alliance Manager, receives reports and gives feedback and comment. However, it is her manager who sits on the Alliance Leadership Team, so this feels like a reversal of the usual practice.

There is a risk here that, as the dialogue is with the Alliance Manager directly rather than the Alliance Leadership Team, this could substitute for or interfere with the latter's role. It is important the Alliance Leadership Team takes the lead on performance monitoring and reporting, flagging any issues up to the Commissioner as Owner if needed. Potentially this is reversed in County Durham if issues are flagged in the one-to-one meeting and taken back to the Alliance Leadership Team for action. To that alliance's credit though, the arrangement appears to work well.

Alliance Leadership Team

The ALT undertakes the governance functions of the alliance. It is the Board, and the main difference from a corporate Board is that it exists solely to deliver the activities and outcomes set by the commissioner for this alliance. In all other respects it has the same governance functions:

- living and promoting the alliance's purpose, principles, values, objectives and outcomes
- establishing and ensuring implementation of its strategic leadership and direction
- creating accountability and management structures to achieve the strategy and outcomes with resources available
- allocating resources to achieve the strategy and outcomes
- ensuring that outcomes are being achieved.

The duties of the ALT do not include getting involved with the day-to-day management of the alliance or allowing individual participants' interests, viewpoints or positions to be promoted.

Alliance Leadership Team members

Being part of the leadership of an innovative and exciting alliance is a privilege and opportunity. You will have a major influence on the alliance and will, rightly, take pride in its success. It is not always easy though. Since around 2014 we have learned a lot about ALTs and how to make them work well. There are many aspects and different issues that may arise. Sometimes being an ALT member can feel amazing, and sometimes tough.

Multiple aspects of ALT membership

The ALT representative role is multi-faceted. This makes it rewarding, but also means that you can sometimes feel as if you are between a rock and hard place. Firstly, an ALT member is there by authority of the commissioner. Secondly, you're there by authority of your own organisation or, in the case of some members, a group you are representing. These authorities mean you are there for a purpose; you have responsibilities to those authorising you and you need to act in their interests. This can only work if their interests are aligned because, if that alignment is absent or weak, your role is near impossible.

You are also a representative. An ALT member represents their own organisation or group in the alliance and also represents the alliance back in their own organisation or group. You are championing your organisation when you're in alliance meetings; and, when back at base, you are championing the alliance.

These four aspects can sometimes pull in different directions, and each ALT member has to manage these tensions and conflicts. There may be times when it is hard to explain to your own organisation what is happening in the alliance. There may be hostility or disinterest and you feel defensive. At other times, you want to do right by organisation but are part of a conversation and decision whereby there will be significant impacts that you know will not play out well or go unchallenged back at base.

It's impossible to avoid tensions completely. The best way to minimise them is to ensure that there is alignment between success for the alliance and success for your organisation.

Commissioner ALT representatives

The commissioner's second role, as alliance participant, is embodied by the commissioner representative on the Alliance Leadership Team. This role is the same as provider organisation representatives. Everyone has equal responsibility to govern and ensure the alliance is as successful as possible.

The commissioner ALT representative is often a senior person with good content knowledge of the service area and local context. They will attend all meetings as an equal participant and contribute to collaborative decision making. They often have good insight into the system-wide issues and links to other commissioner departments. This can be very helpful in unblocking issues and creating new cross-organisational working.

Obviously, as they are keeping their own organisation informed and updated about the alliance, they will be involved in briefing back, although this should be through updates rather than any contract monitoring function. To make this even clearer, we strongly advise that formal reporting from the alliance to the Commissioner as Owner should be through the Chair of the ALT only and not through the commissioner ALT representatives. This helps maintain the separation of their role from that of Commissioner as Owner.

Provider ALT representatives

The provider ALT representative will usually be a senior member of their organisation. As they will need to make decisions on behalf of their organisation, it should be someone who has the necessary delegated authority, typically a Chief Executive or Director. We find the biggest issue for ALT members is time as meetings are often weekly in the first few months, although they then drop to fortnightly or monthly. There is a lot to do in bidding for and then setting up an alliance, so this time commitment needs to be considered when deciding who the ALT representative will be for each organisation.

Advisory or associate members

In other sectors, it is usual for only those with 'skin in the game' to make decisions at ALT level, which is linked to their use of gainshare and painshare in how they structure the financial framework for any alliance. There is more reliance on commercial motives for collaboration.

In the UK public sector we have found that those wanting to work in an alliance already have a strong motivation to collaborate. The commercial aspects matter but are not the main or only reason organisations want to be part of an alliance.

We also recognise that other people, especially those with lived experiences, bring insights, wisdom and value to any decision making. We have therefore adapted the alliance approach to include additional members in ALTs as associate or advisory members. There are often discussions about representation and how best to achieve this. I won't rehearse all the arguments here, but just reiterate that those with lived experience can offer perspectives that would otherwise be absent in a roomful of people with service and delivery roles.

Advisory and associate members will obviously have to adhere to the alliance principles and be focused on success of the alliance. They may be people who attend for one, a few or every meeting. The commissioner and provider ALT members decide what will best help them in their role.

Sometimes the issue of voting or non-voting status comes up. Our preferred route is to avoid the distinction. If the ALT is to make a unanimous, best for people using services decision it is highly unlikely they will do so against the advice of their advisory or associate members. If the latter do not agree with a decision, this needs addressing rather than just saying it doesn't matter as they cannot vote anyway.

Deputies

It is important to have named deputies who can attend meetings with the same delegated authority of the equivalent ALT member. They will need to be familiar with the alliance and its way of working, and kept up to date with developments and issues.

ALT Chair

A Chairperson for meetings will be needed. This should be chosen by the ALT members, and can be one of them or an external appointment. We have examples of both models, with pros and cons. The County Durham Alliance strongly valued its independent Chair during the initial years. Similarly, in Stockport they had an independent chair initially but then found they did not need one later on as everyone became used to the alliance principles. In other alliances, an independent Chair has not worked so well, usually due to being unfamiliar or uncomfortable with the alliance way of working.

Our one stipulation is that the Chair should not be a commissioner ALT member or someone appointed directly by the commissioner. This is to avoid falling back on to the commissioner being the controlling influence. The Chair's role is important in ensuring the alliance principles are upheld. The role is predominantly facilitative, at times helping the group navigate difficult conversations while adhering to the principles and values. It will be someone who understands the need for equality between all partners and best for person, unanimous decision making. The Chair will provide much-needed support to the Alliance Manager, especially in negotiating the complexity and uncertainty that comes with the role.

Conflicts of interest

A quick word on conflicts of interest, which are no different in an alliance to those in any other Board or governance model. There are two types – personal and organisational – where either an individual or an organisation has a direct stake in any action, decision or determination to be taken or made by the ALT. Clearly, you could argue that everyone has a stake in everything as this is an alliance. In practice, potential conflicts usually relate to the award of subcontracts or where one member is keen to take on the work. That organisation's representatives will usually recuse themselves from the process, leaving their colleagues to be the decision makers.

ALT decision making

Decision making in the ALT epitomises the alliance way of working. It is equal, unanimous and focused on best for people. It is true collaboration, namely:

- making decisions together
- implementing those decisions
- being jointly accountable for the results.

These are the elements we use to highlight the difference between talking together and collaborating. If you think about the many meetings you go to that are badged as partnership, alliance or collaboration, how much time do they spend make decisions and jointly sharing in their implementation? Do they see themselves as jointly accountable for the result, or is that considered the responsibility of the party that brings the proposal and leads the implementation?

Of course, there are some excellent examples of cross-organisational groups; but there are also a lot of examples of so-called joint working that are in fact little more than talking shops.

Collaborative decision making works best if everyone comes with ideas and perspectives but, importantly, an open mind. Differences of view can be discussed and the conversations will be rich and informative. One sign of a truly collaborative group is when the discussion leads to an idea or solution that no one had thought of before entering the room. It was only possible when the thoughts, ideas and suggestions from different perspectives were pooled.

There are a couple of key ingredients to enable collaborative decision making – delegated authority and unanimity.

Delegated authority

Delegated authority to make decisions is the key to 'making decisions together'. You cannot come to a decision and then someone says they cannot endorse it until they have taken it back to their Board. The people in the room have to be the decision makers – then and there.

Understanding and establishing the delegated authority are key parts of setting up an alliance. Each representative appointed to the ALT must be authorised to represent and bind the participant organisation they represent on any matter relating to the alliance and the Agreement. Where any substitutes, alternates or deputies attend an ALT meeting, they must have the same powers.

The delegated authority will need to be confirmed by the member organisations' Boards or Trustees. Any limits to that delegation need to be defined and shared in advance of the alliance commencing. Sometimes, schemes of delegation for host organisations need to be altered when they become a member of an alliance that represents a significant part of their business.

All of this is much easier if there is alignment between the vision and aims of the member organisations and the alliance. Put another way, the ALT representative is in an impossible position if there is no alignment and no delegated authority in the room.

Unanimity

People will only be willing to 'implement those decisions' and be 'jointly accountable for results' if they believe the decision was the right one. When I talk to people about alliances, I am commonly asked about unanimous decision making. We all have experience of meetings that become heated discussions as participants take a strong stand and refuse to budge. Sometimes it can be on a point of principle, sometimes clear self-interest. It's hard to visualise how such a group could come to a unanimous position.

Also, people are used to voting and the decision going with the majority vote. We are used to accepting that we cannot always agree. The trouble with majority voting is that, by definition, some people will not agree with the decision. Yes, you can have norms that say that once decision is made everyone is expected to get behind it; but there is often disgruntlement or even sabotage when it comes to putting the decision into practice.

Voting also raises the prospect of shareholder stake, with larger organisations or those with more money at stake wanting a larger share of the vote. With unanimous decision making, all members effectively have an equal voice.

Differences of opinion and even disagreements are fine if you can work through them. Indeed, they are positive and a healthy sign that there is no group think in the alliance. You need to work through and come to a common position. Keep talking, keep open minds, keep looking for the common ground and what you agree on; and, importantly, keep coming back to the purpose, reminding yourselves about the common goal and why you are together.

It might take several conversations or meetings. My most stark example is a difficult financial risk issue with an imminent hard deadline. We had five meetings in a fortnight with very senior people in order to work through, revise the proposed decision, and review and revise it again. We got there.

Continued dialogue and commitment to finding a solution in this case was far better than a majority vote leaving one or more people not agreeing with the decision. A relentless focus on the common goal and the outcomes that demonstrate you have been successful will help. For all major decisions, we recommend you ask three questions:

* Will this decision help us achieve our outcomes?
* Are we adhering to the Alliance Principles?
* Are we adhering to our alliance values?

In this way, self-interest is not even a consideration; it is all about people and achieving what the alliance has been set up to do.

Specific ALT tasks and responsibilities

Each alliance will determine the roles and responsibilities for its own teams, so the following suggestions are just for starters.

Provide strategic direction and leadership for the alliance

The ALT should create, review and renew strategies and plans, ensuring they are focused on achieving its objectives and outcomes. In all these, the ALT provides the leadership necessary, both within the alliance and within their own organisation(s), to allow the alliance to achieve its objectives and outcomes, including nurturing and maintaining support for the alliance.

Set governance frameworks

The ALT is responsible for creating the governance mechanisms for the alliance, including policies, performance reporting and review cycles and any management systems needed. The ALT meetings replace contract monitoring meetings. Instead of monitoring against the terms of a contract, everyone is relentlessly focused on best performance against the alliance objectives and outcomes.

Determine alliance accountabilities and structure

Early tasks include appointment of the Alliance Manager and identification of members of the Alliance Management Team and any other structures for operations. Thereafter the ALT will direct, empower and support them in delivering the alliance objectives and outcomes.

Set ALT operational procedures

The ALT needs to be functioning well for the alliance to be successful. There will be practical issues such as meeting times, frequency, place and minutes preparation, as well as ways of working and reaching decisions together in a way that adheres to the Alliance Principles and values.

Act on the commissioner's directions and report to the commissioner

The relationship with the Commissioner as Owner needs to be established. Early agreement is needed on the reporting content and, from then on, the regular cycle of reports on finance and performance against the alliance outcomes.

Review ALT performance

It is helpful to build in a plan for review and ALT health checks (see Chapter 8), constantly checking that the Alliance Principles are being acted on.

Other governance groups

An organisation of equivalent size to most alliances will have other mechanisms for assurance and accountability, such as committees for finance, remuneration, clinical governance, health and safety. Most larger alliances have separate finance committees instructed by and reporting to the ALT, while smaller alliances rely on dedicated finance resources working alongside the Alliance Manager.

In order to minimise duplication of other functions, it may be possible to use the set-up in one member organisation to provide oversight for alliance activity. For instance, a Clinical Governance Group in an NHS Trust might be able to expand its remit to review clinical governance elements for an alliance to which it belongs.

Alliance Management Team

The AMT is the driving force for delivery across the alliance, running and co-ordinating it day to day. Working as an integrated, collaborative body, the AMT can capitalise on the relationships between members and remove organisational barriers.

The AMT is not a strategic decision making one: it puts into practice the strategies set by the Alliance Leadership Team, which directs the AMT on the delivery plans and then delegates decisions about implementation to it. The AMT will also have an important co-ordination role in making sure activities between and across member organisations run smoothly. Depending on the alliance and its areas of activity, the AMT may be in contact daily or may meet weekly. Its key roles can be summarised as:

* living and promoting the alliance's purpose, principles, values, objectives and outcomes
* co-ordinating and managing the delivery of support and services, meeting or exceeding the alliance objectives and outcomes
* developing and implementing plans as directed by the ALT
* reporting on performance for the ALT
* providing day-to-day management and leadership to the wider alliance teams.

Alliance Management Team members

The AMT is set up by the ALT and is accountable to it. The ALT decides the size and composition of the AMT, and may review and change this over time as the alliance progresses. AMT members should be experienced managers from member organisations who have the appropriate expertise and experience to make key operational decisions within the alliance. They should have a good understanding of its objectives and outcomes and be able to focus on achieving those outcomes rather than delivering a process.

The AMT is a management and delivery group rather than a representative one: it does not need to include a member from every alliance member organisation or equal numbers from each organisation. All members of the AMT are appointed on merit as the best person for the job to create a fully integrated team. It is unlikely to include a member from the commissioner organisation, although one or two alliances do so for specific reasons.

Job descriptions for AMT members should include not only their individual line management roles but also their collective AMT management role.

Specific tasks and responsibilities

These typically include the following:

1. Promotion of the alliance way of working – such as vision, purpose, objectives, values and behaviours. The AMT must be seen to be acting at all times in accordance with these, which might include consideration of developing the alliance culture and how this is cascaded through the alliance.
2. Workforce plans – such as developing job descriptions and appointing and inducting alliance personnel.
3. Services Operations Manual – this contains key policy and procedure information available to all alliance teams that the AMT develops, maintains and reviews.
4. Delivery – the AMT implements the management/delivery plan that will deliver the alliance objectives and outcomes, and should review performance against the plan and take all actions necessary to deliver the required performance.
5. Performance reporting – the AMT produces accurate, complete and timely reports for the ALT. The content should be developed with the ALT and amended as necessary to be relevant over the duration of the alliance.
6. Internal communications – the AMT should develop and implement an internal communications strategy and plan for the alliance and its subcontractors. The effectiveness of this strategy should be measured through surveys and data collection and the plans reviewed as necessary.

Other management and co-ordination groups

Every alliance operates in its own context and will have different internal arrangements. Typically we see a number of working groups feeding into the AMT. One of our larger alliances includes another tier of operational co-ordination, leaving the AMT with a more innovation or change programme-type focus.

The Plymouth Alliance has a different arrangement altogether, and now operates without an Alliance Manager or Alliance Management Team. This is in part due to early recruitment difficulties which meant they had to find a way to operate without the Alliance Manager. They therefore set up subgroups: three for services (accommodation, substance use and treatment, and children and young people); and three for running the alliance (communications, governance and finance). Each is led by an ALT member and meets regularly. This worked well for them, so they decided to continue without an Alliance Manager – although they have a dedicated full-time Business Support Officer and part-time Finance Officer in place.

It may take a while to settle on the arrangements that work. Different functions and focus will be needed in the early months of each alliance compared with the more steady state after the first year or so. The only rule is to keep things as lean as possible while creating enough capacity and headroom to co-ordinate effectively and be able to focus on achieving the alliance objectives and outcomes.

Alliance Managers or Directors

The Alliance Manager leads the alliance. For a larger alliance, the role is a Director-level one. There are Alliance Directors in several of the alliances we have set up, reflecting the level of complexity and amount of responsibility involved.

For simplicity, I will use the term 'Alliance Manager' but throughout, this refers to Alliance Manager or Alliance Director. The Alliance Manager is the 'go to' person for all alliance matters. They are, as people, the glue that holds it together. It is a key role, similar to a Chief Operating Officer (COO). However, unlike a COO in a single organisation, an Alliance Manager has to work across a number of organisations. Even with the most supportive ALT members who understand fully the alliance way of working, the Alliance Manager will sometimes find themselves navigating through opposing views and different styles and time frames for decision making.

The Alliance Manager leads the AMT and attends ALT meetings. They are appointed by the ALT and are accountable to it. The attributes needed to undertake the role range from operational and people management through to negotiation and facilitation skills. It is therefore important to take time to make sure you have the right person for the role. Due to the pressing need to appoint someone early on in order to make progress, we recommend an interim Alliance Manager who can be in place for the first months, year or even two years of an alliance. This allows new alliances to identify someone who has strong programme management skills to be able to get the alliance up and running.

Time can be taken for recruitment of a permanent Alliance Manager for the next phases where, alongside project management, strong relationship-building and maintenance are key attributes. Clarity about the requirements for the role, accountabilities and support will help with successful recruitment. The impact of the role is illustrated in this example from Camden.

Alliance in practice – Camden Mental Health Resilience Alliance

This launched with an interim Alliance Manager in place following initial difficulties recruiting someone to take on the role permanently.

> The Alliance described how the appointee was instrumental in bringing it together and galvanising it. It was during her tenure that the Lived Experience Advisers were appointed. Unfortunately, she moved to another role, so there was a period without an Alliance Manager.
>
> Not surprisingly, there was a sense of ebb and flow of energy and attention to the Alliance during those early years. They describe how someone with a full-time role at the centre of the Alliance changes how involved people feel. The tone, morale and importance people place on the Alliance is dependent on that leadership role.

Most Alliance Managers and Directors are full time, and in some cases already work for one of the member organisations. Initially, they may have to proactively manage the shift in people's perception that they are now an alliance worker rather than a worker in a specific member organisation. Over time, this will not be an issue. Obviously, this is harder if they work part time with the alliance and part time in their previous role – not impossible but probably best avoided.

Alliance Managers in practice

Some years ago we interviewed Flora Henderson about her role as Alliance Manager of the Future Pathways Alliance in Scotland – one she had held for four years at the time. Flora had previously worked in the non-profit sector and in international development and humanitarian roles.

Flora Henderson's reflections on being an Alliance Manager

The role

My role is pretty varied. Some parts are akin to other management roles I've had, for example, about the demands of negotiating a direction, sometimes with a range of partners. Particularly when the programmes is complex, where the environment is changeable, and there are different needs and interests, the best way forward can be hard to discern.

It's about working to determine that direction and supporting your team members to deliver their part of it. Working with an Alliance Leadership Team can feel similar to working with a board of directors in the need to sustain focus on strategy, governance and performance.

Perhaps the difference is that I don't necessarily manage the team I lead. I see this as an advantage. I wouldn't say it's always smooth, there's always improvement available, but alliancing encourages colleagues to draw on a wider set of resources. This means that we can access support, expertise, training would otherwise be unavailable. And that benefits the work.

I also really value access to our funder and partner the Scottish Government. I might seek their procurement advice, an area where Commissioners tend to have a lot of experience. This dialogue and advice was integral to our Alliance becoming able to confidently work with numbers of delivery partners. They might seek the Alliance's input, providing opportunities for the Alliance to shape future policy and services by sharing what we have learned about what people need, and where barriers may still exist. Being able to develop our contribution to the future of services is an aspiration, as Future Pathways is the first service of its kind.

Positives

I have really enjoyed my role and the reason I've enjoyed it is because we have been able to do work in a new way and make a visible difference to numbers of people who have not been well served by professionals in the past. We have learned a lot about who we are working with, what is important to them and what it takes to deliver high quality support.

I am well supported by my colleagues across the different organisations. We have worked through some genuinely difficult issues over the years. It can be hard to arrive at agreement at times, some things might feel unsolvable, but I do think there's a great benefit in the principle of consensual decision making and creating additional space for that.

The multidisciplinary approach has so much to recommend it and a form of partnership that allows those different and diverse perspectives to be present and help inform the work is really helpful.

Challenges

We've learnt a lot about where to invest our time. One of the challenges in our particular alliance is that we've got partners from very different backgrounds. There are some relatively small non profit partners and large statutory partners, the NHS Greater Glasgow and Clyde and the Scottish Government.

Each of our partners will bring its own perspective, culture and beliefs about how things work. I think we might have put more time in is our policy alignment. Not on everything because that's overwhelming and unhelpful, but certainly in the area of complaints and governance, that part is really worth some concentrated thought, bearing in mind that the legal underpinning of the alliance is a contract, not charity or public body legislation as it might be another context. It's not a problem but it is an area where it's worth spending some time.

Advice for others

Take your time

I would say take your time and build your relationships. Try not to be too quick. We did a lot quickly particularly at the start of the project and the time you invest in planning pays dividends. I think trying to rush the start can be difficult. Think early about continuity and how you might induct newcomers, both at the ALT and operationally. There will be change.

I think my personal learning has been about slowing down and just making sure you've got the right information, the support that you need from other people, taking that extra bit of time, when sometimes it feels like, that's the last thing you have.

Focus on relationships

The relationship is probably the most important aspect, particularly in this work. You're seeking to usually solve a complex problem, the answers unknown and you're looking to have support of your core partners but often a wider set of stakeholders in addition to that. That relational approach is fundamental to doing this.

Alliance Managers' core team

We talk regularly with Alliance Managers and Alliance Directors around the country. When a new person joins the group, we ask everyone to give them some gems of advice: what they wish they had known at the beginning, what they wish they had done early on. Without fail, they mention getting administrative and other help. There is so much to do at the launch of an alliance, and it all falls to the Alliance Manager. Without support, they are covering everything: from booking meeting rooms to developing copy for communications;

from meeting stakeholders, some of whom will be quite suspicious and concerned, to developing performance and finance reports.

Administration, communications and finance support are the three priorities. The latter two do not have to be full-time posts. Typically, specific people from the member organisations are identified and take on the role for a set number of sessions per week or per month. Funding for these posts will need to come from the funding allocation or other sources. Often additional 'start-up' funds are allocated for the first year or two, but thereafter the funding will revert to the alliance.

Troubleshooting

Collaboration isn't always easy. Working together brings a lot of benefits, but there is a flip side. Getting everyone on board can take time, slow things down. There can be vested interests or suspicion about vested interests.

Here we discuss some of the things that can cause problems or take time to settle down. Even when they have arisen, the issues can be worked through. They are not showstoppers, just things to anticipate and avoid or to recognise quickly and resolve.

Commissioner role on the ALT

The ALT or Shadow ALT is formed once the provider members are confirmed. It will have representatives from the provider member organisations, the commissioning organisations and associates, often people who use the relevant services. As the ALT comes together, especially after a competitive procurement process, there are a number of factors to recognise:

- The providers have often gelled as a group as they prepared a bid and went through the evaluation process; they have formed, stormed and normed.
- The commissioner representative is likely to be someone who was an evaluator in the procurement process; they move from judge to colleague.
- The commissioner representative is likely to be someone with in-depth knowledge and experience of the subject area as well as the wider strategy – someone who is used to having a lot of control.

It is likely to take a while for a sense of equality and unanimity to be realised. People will be used to the commissioner having the final say. The commissioner will have to let that go, and the providers need to avoid looking to the commissioner to make the final decisions. It needs work on both sides. The following do's and don'ts might help:

- Don't make the commissioner representative Chair of the ALT. Although the Chair's role in an alliance is one of facilitation rather than leadership, the Chair convenes and runs meetings, so people look to it for direction.

- Make sure the Chair is the one who formally reports to the Commissioner as Owner, who is represented by a person who is not the commissioner representative on the ALT. The latter is not there to represent that owner role other than to help the alliance achieve its objectives and outcomes. The commissioner representative on the ALT is not there to be the voice of the Commissioner as Owner.
- If you are the commissioner representative, make sure you don't dominate conversations or hold on to information you have. You need to recognise the expertise of others, often depth rather than breadth. Go into meetings with a mindset that says you don't know what the answer is. Don't go in thinking your role is to persuade others to agree to what you want to happen.
- If you are a provider representative, make room for the commissioner to join the group. Make them feel welcome and valued as an equal and a colleague. Avoid looking to the commissioner representative to close discussions or have the final say on a decision.
- Do something special to mark the 'closure' of the old relationship and the 'opening' of the new.

ALT Overinvolvement in detail

It is important there is a clear distinction between the governance role of the Alliance Leadership Team and the management role of the Alliance Management Team. One of the commonest issues I see when I undertake a six-month 'health check' for an alliance is that the ALT and AMT are overlapping too much. For example, the AMT is sending things to the ALT for decision or approval, and the ALT is covering too many minor issues. The agendas for their meetings can then look quite similar.

This happens because of circumstances; it isn't anyone's fault. As an alliance develops, often only one or two people per member organisation are involved. They may have been meeting as a bid team, and each will know a lot about the bid, delivery plans and finances. Usually, they are senior personnel in their organisations, often Chief Executives.

When the alliance forms these are often the people who will be on the Alliance Leadership Team. They will identify others in their organisation to be involved in running the alliance day to day. Finding or appointing those people will take time. The result is that, in the early months, there is often the ALT and little else. An Alliance Manager may not be in place; instead, the ALT members are doing everything and are very knowledgeable about all the details and nuances. Hopefully, before long, the Alliance Management Team and other key roles are filled, at which point the ALT can step back.

The secret to this is to have a high level of trust in the AMT to deliver on its responsibilities and adhere to the alliance principles and values. The ALT should give clear direction and then delegate detailed decisions to the AMT without the need for checking or interference. This can take a while to establish, with the ALT learning to let go of the detail while the AMT develops its own expertise. To help, we use the following exercise early in the life of an alliance. It is a useful one to repeat at intervals, especially if there is a sense that the lines between both teams are becoming blurred.

Workshop exercise – ALT and AMT offers and expectations

Soon after the formation of the alliance and after appointing the Alliance Manager and Alliance Management Team, hold a joint ALT and AMT session.

The ALT and the AMT go into separate rooms. Each composes a letter to the other team. In it they set out their offer to the other team and their expectations of the other team.

Come back together as a joint group and exchange letters. Get someone to read out the one you have received. As a group, discuss the ideas and suggestions.

Agree what this means in practice; how you will check you are keeping to the ideas; and what you will do if you think you are not putting the commitments into practice.

Here are a few other tips to help:

- The delegated authority from the Commissioner as Owner to the alliance needs to be reflected throughout the alliance. The ALT must delegate decisions about the everyday running of the alliance to the AMT. It can give the AMT some parameters for that, but then it should stand back.
- The AMT will have the same decision-making criteria so there can be trust in the AMT to consider:
  o Will this decision help us achieve our outcomes?
  o Does it adhere to our principles?
  o Does it adhere to our values?
- If you find the AMT is sending papers 'for approval', stop and ask whether that is needed. If the issue is being worked through according to the three criteria above, why does it need a second opinion?
- Set the ALT agenda to one-third strategy (the future), one-third performance (the past) and one-third current issues (the present). In that way, the latter does not dominate.

Alliance Manager and Alliance Director burnout

The role of the Alliance Manager or Alliance Director is never an easy one. Even when the alliance governance is well set up, everyone is clear about their roles and responsibilities and there is minimal duplication, there will be difficult days. If the governance is not working well, most days will be difficult. If you add to this a lack of or confusing line management support, along with no team around you, you can see why the role could become impossible.

It is hard to stress enough how critical it is for the role of Alliance Manager or Director to be well thought through, including their supervision and support and the team around them. Then you need to recruit the right person. We have already talked about finding an interim while you take time to undertake a full recruitment. It may also take more than one go to find the right person for such a key role.

People leaving and being replaced

A group is always disrupted when people leave or new ones arrive, but it is inevitable that people will change jobs during the lifetime of the alliance. If it is someone who has been involved from the very beginning, maybe even before it came into being, they will have a lot of organisational memory which will potentially be lost. At the very least, it will change the skills and knowledge mix in the group.

Change can and should be positive, but there will be an inevitable period of settling in for new people. Again, some tips:

- If you are new to the alliance, find out as much as possible about developments to date. Speak to people about their role in the story so far. Read up about alliancing and alliance contracting. Don't assume you know about alliances; find out about this one.
- If someone new is coming into your alliance, make sure they have an induction period in the same way as a new employee. Give them information about alliancing and alliance contracting in general and specifics about your alliance.
- Assume it will take 3–4 months for the group to settle down again.

Difficulties reaching unanimous decisions

Some decisions are hard to make, even if you keep the focus on 'best for people' because we can have different views on what is 'best for people'. This is where having people with lived experiences in the room can help, as will a strong commitment to thinking about support and services from the perspective of people rather than services.

Here are a few tips for getting through thorny issues:

- Keep talking in the room; avoid conversations in corridors with one or two people unless these are precursors to going back into the room with fresh ideas.
- Keep reminding each other of the elements you agree on and specify those you don't. Talk through the latter and, as you resolve them, the disagreement list will get shorter and shorter until it disappears.
- If you are a lone voice against a potential decision, reflect on whether this is related to a concern or aspiration for your own organisation. If it genuinely is not, keep talking, explaining why you disagree. Don't resort to agreeing just to help move things on.
- If someone is disagreeing, find out what lies behind that. If it is genuinely related to 'best for people', think about how you can adapt the proposed decision to take this perspective into account. It might mean phasing in a change or testing in a small way first rather than a big bang, for instance.
- If the discussions are getting heated, be conscious of how you are interacting. Are you adhering to your values, are you treating others with respect, are your allowing everyone space? It may help to take time out or invite an independent observer to your meetings.
- Keep talking.

Decisions not being carried through

This is usually only a potential issue in the early days when you are mobilising an alliance and not everyone is in place. When few people have dedicated time to the alliance outside of their existing job, it is not surprising that actions from a meeting are not implemented. My tips here are mostly about capacity. To avoid delays in actioning decisions:

- Appoint or identify an Alliance Manager early, using an interim Manager in the pre- and early days of an alliance. There is an enormous amount to do and you need someone full time to make things happen.
- Identify a small team to support the Alliance Manager as soon as possible.
- Identify administrative support for the Alliance Manager.
- Be realistic and clear on action points for the Alliance Manager and Alliance Management Team, then leave them to get on with it.

If the delay or lack of action is not related to capacity, it might be an issue of commitment, which we will discuss in the next section.

Unequal contributions from alliance members

We have talked about how critical it is for all members of the alliance to be committed to its way of working, to the alliance principles, and we discussed the dangers of unequal commitment. This might manifest itself in different ways, such as non-attendance at meetings, lack of input, the adoption of entrenched positions or lack of action in carrying through unanimously agreed decisions.

Hopefully you will have chosen partners carefully and openly discussed your common goals (alignment), agreed to ways of working (commitment) and had frank conversations about what you all want to get from the alliance and what you can bring (value creation). If difficulties arise, especially around commitment to the alliance principles, you will need to air the issue and find a constructive way forward. The earlier you do this the better, to prevent assumptions and bad feeling from developing. In extreme circumstances, you may need to consider whether the member organisation is really able or willing to be committed to the alliance way of working.

Summary

Following the tried and tested alliance governance model will enable you to share responsibility and decision making while maximising people's time. Clarity of roles within the model and adherence to the alliance principles will help avoid or minimise some of the common problems. Collaboration, while rewarding, is not always easy. Building trust and facing difficult moments together will allow your collaboration to grow and strengthen.

In the next chapter we will look at how this sense of togetherness is conveyed to others and the benefits of acting as one spreads to everyone working in the alliance.

Reference

Nielsen, B. (2010). Strategic fit, contractual and procedural governance in alliances. *Journal of Business Research*, *63*, 682–689. https://doi.org/10.1016/j.jbusres.2009.05.001.

Case study 6

The Plymouth Alliance (2019–present)

The Plymouth Alliance is focused on people facing multiple disadvantage and homelessness in the Devon city. It aims to enable people to fulfil their potential, support them to become independent and help them achieve their goals. It is working closely with Plymouth City Council's teams, who perform the statutory council functions in relation to homelessness.

Creating the Alliance

In Plymouth, there had long been a drive to move to an approach based on purpose, relationships and learning together. The Council had already set up a series of groups of providers who were meeting regularly to look at whole-system improvements on different topics. One group was focused on those with disadvantages, whether related to homelessness, drug and alcohol misuse, mental health issues or offending. The group was made up of organisations with a long history of working together in the city.

Plymouth City Council and the NHS had set up integrated commissioning in the late 2010s, and the Director of Integrated Commissioning at the time picked up on alliancing as a way to create further integration and collaboration. The Plymouth Alliance went live in April 2019 following a procurement and negotiation period that commenced in June 2018, and comprises seven members in addition to the council. The contract was for five years with options to extend to up to ten years, the next two years of which have been confirmed, and annual funding was £7.7 million for year one.

Progress of the Alliance

Much has happened in its first five years, and those involved are unequivocal that working as an alliance has allowed them to do things that would not otherwise be possible. Their speed of response during the pandemic meant they were able to house people at very short notice rather than move them into hotels. They have put in new support, from small things such as free vapes (e-cigarettes) through to new mixed teams who bring expertise from different organisations.

Fundamentally, the Alliance has allowed them to be flexible and try out new ideas without having to seek permission each time. Having no detailed specification has meant they are not micromanaged against a historic description of their services. The empowerment from the council to the Alliance is also mirrored internally, with managers and staff who will spontaneously implement new ways of working. There is a culture of innovation along with an acceptance of failure as a learning opportunity.

Members of the Plymouth Alliance rightly stress that their philosophy and relationships are what have made the difference. The contract is just a vehicle, albeit one that amplified their ambition. As Gary Wallace from Public Health at Plymouth City Council describes it, 'the alliance contract we put in place had a symbolic impact in opening minds and therefore opening doors'.

All this could potentially be achieved without an alliance, but would be harder. There is also the recognition that it is not always easy and that time, capacity and resources are needed to run the Alliance. However, it has helped move collaboration and innovation to be the default rather than the exception. There is a strong culture of empowering staff to try new ideas, putting them into practice without seeking permission. While there remains a strong sense of identity for each member organisation, their individual workforces also feel a part of the wider whole, the Alliance.

Within the Alliance experiences may still differ. Small local organisations sit alongside large corporates that operate in other geographical areas. They have had to learn about each other and adapt. External factors have had differential impacts on different members. For instance, organisations involved in accommodation have been affected more by the housing crisis than those who provide support and services.

Differences are valued however, and everyone recognises the sense of safety in numbers. In the fiscal reality of the UK public sector recently, some services may have lost funding and some organisations potentially fold. Being part of an alliance in itself means that hasn't happened.

The observations of the senior commissioner who joined the ALT after a few years of the Alliance are interesting. She helped bring expertise and capacity around subcontracting as well as financial governance and oversight. As someone who joined the Alliance later on, she is enthusiastic about the levels of trust and transparency between everyone and how, as a collective, they make decisions and share insights, risk and resources. They bid together for other grants and funding and, more often than not, are successful.

One of the reflections from Plymouth is the need to adapt over time. The requirements and skill sets you need at the beginning to get up and running are different to those you need later on. The flexibility built into alliancing allows changes and adjustments to be made.

In Plymouth there is pride in the Alliance and this, along with the longer contract length, has given the organisations involved confidence and stability. People can focus on their core purpose and do their best for the citizens of Plymouth, rather than worry about their own organisation's survival.

As with the other longstanding alliances, those involved in Plymouth still reference the Alliance Principles as pivotal to the way they work. These, along with the values specific to this alliance, have shaped all they have achieved and have been written into its Charter and subcontracts.

It is striking in the Plymouth Alliance how much their philosophy was already there and it extends beyond the Alliance. Each member has other services not formally part of the Alliance, and there are shared activities with non-partner organisations. The sense of collaboration and sharing training and resources permeates everything. The Alliance Agreement, as it should, is supporting the way of working, not creating it.

What changed for people

Nicola Greenfield, Head of Homelessness, Health and Wellbeing for BCHA, a charitable housing association member of the Alliance, has been on the Alliance Leadership Team since the outset. She works across other areas of Southwest England and says: 'You can see the difference in Plymouth compared with other places. It is liberating, we are not limited by a specification, we can respond quickly to changing need and try things. And it gets results.'

Since the start of the Alliance, hundreds of people have been supported, used its facilities and services and been housed. Accommodation units have increased in numbers and co-ordinated access to temporary accommodation and support is provided. More recently services have seen increasing numbers of families facing homelessness, and the Alliance was able to respond with resources to fund a team to support families while they were in temporary accommodation and move them into permanent accommodation.

For more information see: https://theplymouthalliance.co.uk/.

6   Alliance culture

If an alliance is best thought of as a virtual organisation, how do those working in it feel part of a single entity when they work for different organisations? Do they need to? Many people are well used to working in mixed teams, matrix structures and multiple partnerships, often at the same time. We wear different hats at different times, knowing which one to put on when and where.

It is possible to create a strong alliance identity and culture without compromising that of each organisation. A balance can be found between pride in one's own organisation and all that it does within and outside of the alliance and a shared unified pride in the alliance. The one strengthens the other, and vice versa.

In this chapter we look ways to build the sense of 'one team' within the alliance culture and how a strong identity can help.

Workforce and culture

A colleague once described an alliance training day that was held shortly after she took up her new post in a member organisation. She was new to alliancing as a form of collaboration and was joining an alliance that had been running for several years. As usual, at the beginning of the day, everyone was asked to introduce themselves. All the participants gave their name and said they worked for the alliance. No one used their member organisation role – they all saw themselves as part of the alliance first and foremost. This was very powerful for her and helped her understand the importance of the alliance for people locally.

So how do you create that sense of one team? It is in part about the shared experiences and connections of people working in the alliance, taking individual organisations' histories, values and ways of working to build a collective one. It will take time, and certainly won't happen overnight.

There is a wealth of literature and experience on leadership for collaboration and creating collaborative cultures. Here I will highlight a few practical elements that I have seen in different alliances; ones that seem relatively easy to implement.

DOI: 10.4324/9781003511809-6

Role modelling by senior leaders

As we all know, creating a culture is not a one-off activity, a set of values or an annual awayday exercise. It involves the words and behaviours of everyone every day. The ways in which people speak and act create and maintain the culture over a period of time. This is especially true of senior leaders.

The strongest alliances are those where the senior leaders have a good understanding of both collaboration and their role in fostering collaborative behaviours. They consistently and frequently demonstrate collaborative leadership qualities. You will have your own sense of what those are, but for me they include humility, openness, curiosity and being comfortable with ambiguity and differences of opinion.

A primary function of both Alliance Leadership Team (ALT) and Alliance Management Team (AMT) members is to live the alliance values. This is not a superficial statement, a soft fluffy part of the role. It is absolutely fundamental to your alliance's success. Michelle Hill from Stockport's Prevention Alliance talks about 'generous collaboration', where you give more than you need to on paper. She is one of many people with leadership roles in alliances who talk about the central importance of the Alliance Principles.

Time together

During the course of their work for an alliance, people will obviously spend time together. This creates familiarity and people will naturally get to know each other over time. There will be similarities and also differences, different working cultures and ways of doing things. These differences can cause tension, especially if there is little time because of demand and delivery pressures. Time for people to get together away from the daily pressures should be planned from the very beginning of an alliance, as specific team get-togethers or all-staff awaydays and for a range of purposes. Events that bring people together for learning and training, social occasions and celebrations are all part of creating a sense of community across the alliance. For instance, the Plymouth Alliance actively works to bring staff together and foster a sense of working as one. It holds three-monthly 'Partnerships and Pathways' events to which all staff are invited; there is an alliance newsletter and shared training.

I have seen how powerful it is to bring people together for learning. A good facilitator who uses the experience of the participants and learning from each other as part of the day can create a memorable experience. People will learn not only about a particular topic but also about each other. You could hold a day where the purpose is specifically to build understanding of each other. We have used a 'one-team' workshop model where participants spend time learning about each other's backgrounds and each organisation's history. There are also sessions on shared values and hopes for the future.

Cultural-cognitive expertise and alliances

A recent paper on alliancing resonated with me. Derek Walker is an academic in Australia who publishes on alliances and integrated project delivery in the engineering sector. I often find that his work offered lessons for the UK health and care world even though it is about level-crossing removal programmes and similar. His 2020 paper, 'Transforming Strategy into Action on Integrated Project Delivery (IPD) Projects', has a few gems about the human element of alliances, as shown by its research question and main conclusions.

Research question

Which mechanisms, behaviours and processes actively support integrated project delivery participants to make sense of project governance rules and protocols in a way that enables them to collaborate and forge common goals that results in unified collective action?

Conclusions

1. Personal attributes of project participants are vital, particularly their cultural-cognitive expertise. The evidence on how project teams are selected in alliances for example suggests that care is taken to select team members who demonstrate an open mind, have good perspective taking abilities and the capacity, motivation and ability to collaborate through dialogue to make sense of complex issues.

2. The workplace environment needs to support initiative taking, learning from mistakes, be recognised as having a no-blame culture and have low power and information asymmetry. This enables people to engage in dialogue, free of fear of being punished or not respected for their opinion or position when engaging in dialogue. The workplace needs to present fertile ground for personal and cross-team cultural-cognitive expertise in order to exercise appropriate agency.

3. The contractual form adopted is vital in encouraging and supporting collaboration and dialogue between individuals and teams when making sense of challenges and opportunities resulting from operating regulatory arrangements.

4. Effective cultural-cognitive expertise requires both workplace practice support but also mentoring, training and development to hone collaboration and dialogue enabling skills.

Walker (2020, pp. 3, 18–19; emphasis in original).

The term 'cultural-cognitive expertise' was new to me, but this quote from one of the participants in the research interviews helped me understand what it means in practice:

> You can certainly tell people who, from [Contractor X] or other organisations that come onto the team and have worked in an alliance, because you can just see their ability to want to listen, understand, or try to understand what your motivation is and what your drivers are, versus just being very closed shop and just saying, well this is a driver and that's what we're doing.

Walker's paper details how people move from being cultural-cognitive novices to experts, initially relying on rules and cultural norms when they experience the anxiety and uncertainty of a new situation. As they develop, they become more able to use initiative with rules as a guide. When expert, they immediately grasp both the situational context and cultural influences and can rapidly respond, adapting and even creating new rules.

Of course, the question is then how to help people move from novice to expert. Walker talks about this: 'Enabling people to most effectively apply their cultural-cognitive thinking to guide effective decision making and action relies heavily on the organisational environment encouraging initiative and being supportive' (p. 8).

This brings us back to the practical actions needed to create that organisational environment. We see it in several alliances where there is a strong sense of delegation of responsibility to innovate or make decisions. This is created by the leadership and senior management teams creating a supportive environment and investing in people's development.

Brand and identity

For those outside the alliance, a visible manifestation of collaboration is the brand and associated information. A strong brand with a name, logo and website gives substance to the alliance. Webpages, social media, newsletters and other forms of communication provide information and updates to those who might not otherwise know about the alliance. Most of all, that clear identity makes the alliance real and tangible.

Name

Most of the alliances we have set up attempt to describe the alliance in the name. Some have stuck with a particular name throughout, while others have changed it. Below are two examples.

Lambeth Integrated Personalised Support Alliance

We all admit that this is not a great name if you are looking for something snappy and jargon-free. However it was kept. This alliance provided support and services to people with severe and enduring mental illness in secure accommodation or at risk of being so. 'Integrated personalised support' was a key phrase that the instigators wanted to keep in everyone's minds. On that level, the name was spot on. However 'Integrated Personalised Support Alliance' is a bit of a mouthful, so was always shortened to IPSA. Then, of course, people forgot what the acronym stood for, or it was talked about as the 'IPSA Alliance', repeating the 'Alliance' part.

Another problem was that another 'IPSA' was set up in the UK at around the same time (the Independent Parliamentary Standards Authority) in response to the scandal surrounding Members of Parliament (MPs') expenses – an unfortunate coincidence. We tried to find something punchier, but other terms were either already in use locally or did not explain what the alliance was about. The name stayed.

Looking back, the clunky name didn't preclude a strong identity. It was a very successful alliance and people talk about it with pride. 'The IPSA' may need some explaining to those who have not heard the name, before but to people in the London borough of Lambeth it is associated with positive and groundbreaking achievements.

Future Pathways

By contrast, another successful alliance has a name that does not directly explain what it does. The working title of this alliance was the In Care Survivor Support Fund Service Alliance – which was not kept. When this alliance was launched, the Scottish Government asked the forum of those with lived experiences of in-care abuse to decide on its name. 'Future Pathways' was their choice and was immediately adopted. This is another alliance whose name has become associated with success for the member organisations, including the Scottish Government.

Two different styles of name, both successful; and, 5–7 years later, it does not matter which route they took.

Logo and visual identity

An early conversation in most alliances is how to develop their logo and visual identity. Again, different alliances have taken different approaches. Some have had someone in the alliance design a logo and colours and then used those. Others have included these elements in their website design, but using specialist web designers and developers. One alliance engaged a communications agency to undertake a full brand development, along with values and behaviours. They brought everyone together to discuss the look and feel they wanted the alliance to represent. It was potentially a good group development exercise too.

There is no right or wrong way. It will depend on budgets and timescales. My only suggestion is to make sure it is, in part at least, a collective exercise with those with lived experiences.

Website

A few years ago, we set up a small alliance in one of the London boroughs. It was for children and young people, and involved a number of voluntary sector organisations. As it was a small-value contract and only expected to run for a couple of years (three at most), there was no attempt to develop an identity for the alliance.

I used to have a case study about this alliance on my website. During the years it ran (and after) I had a number of personal phone calls from people wanting to refer young people to the service. The calls were from schools or even from the social work teams of the council that had set up the alliance. For me, this was illuminating. Firstly, the service was something people wanted to access. Secondly, they wanted information about it and how to refer themselves or others; but, on searching the internet, they could only find the case study on my website. I would therefore direct them to a contact from the alliance of course, but it felt like a missed opportunity for the alliance itself. This alliance was not the only one that I took calls about. There were two others where my phone number was found by people local to the alliance searching for a way to make contact.

The common issue here is that none of them had a dedicated website. Yes, there may be a page on a council site or on other local site, or a press release from the time of the launch. But that does not score much on search engine optimisation, so internet searches will not find them easily.

My advice to any new alliance is that the minimum requirement is a standalone webpage with contact details using domain name specific to the alliance. This might, of course, open up other questions about the need for email hosting and compatibility with member organisations platforms. The webpage should have some basic information to help those working in member organisations understand the alliance. It will also tell others about the alliance – the general public, stakeholders, those who might access the support and services, and any other relevant agencies.

Communications

As the alliance develops, you can strengthen the one-team sense by how you communicate internally and externally. As with the brand and website, unified communications are a visible sign of the strength of the collaboration.

Once an alliance is up and running and has its own brand and website, it is usual to have communications and social media activity that are clearly from and about the alliance. This can go as far as surveys, consultations and events that come under the banner of the alliance. This does not mean that there can be no individual organisational communications. There is no right or wrong answer for how much you do as an alliance and how much you do as individual organisations. They can sit beside each other comfortably and, hopefully, not compete.

It is in the early days that issues can arise. We all know that writing and editing by committee is hard, and you want to avoid needing multiple sources of approval for communications. Yet we sometimes find that trust is not yet established enough for people to leave the crafting of communications to others.

In addition, there can be a lot of pressure to let people know that the alliance exists and what it is doing. Some may want to celebrate and tell the world, while others are more cautious and keen to ensure there is common understanding between all members and their own workforces first.

Some alliances bring in external professionals to create initial communications plans and messaging, while others appoint someone from a member organisation. Either way, it is best to be prepared for it to take a little while for different preferences and styles to come together. Having watched a number of alliances form, here are a few tips:

- Identify some capacity for communications, especially in the first six months.
- Spend time confirming a communications plan and timings, and then stick to them.
- Spend time on collective agreement about style, tone and language (phraseology to use and to avoid). Don't allow differences of opinion to surface once someone has been asked to create something with an imminent deadline.
- Beware if some people do not want alliance communications or prefer to unilaterally issue press releases from their own organisation that claim credit for alliance activities. This is a sign of lack of commitment to the collaboration and will cause resentment. If it happens, it must be explored, not ignored.
- Be patient – it will take a while to move from being in control of your own organisation's communications to settling into a collaborative model for your alliance.
- Remember that alliances share reputational risk. Communications are part of managing and mitigating risks, whether proactively or, hopefully rarely, reactively.

Summary

Mature alliances have a strong sense of identity and cohesion. There are no shortcuts to creating the alliance culture. It takes time to develop and is dependent on positive actions, branding, communications and workforce development. It requires strong leadership and proactive ways to bring people together. Recruiting and developing people with high levels of cultural-cognitive competency will help an alliance be successful.

A strong brand identity for your alliance will make it real. A visual brand, along with easily found online resources with information about the alliance, is the minimum. How you develop communications strategies and plans will be specific to each alliance. There are no hard and fast rules. Once you have established your brand and style and have started seeing how the alliance's communications sit alongside those of your own organisation, it will become easier.

Having looked at activities to build identity within an alliance, in the next chapter we turn our attention to relationships outside the alliance.

Reference

Walker, D. (2020). Transforming strategy into action on integrated project delivery (IPD) projects. *Engineering Project Organization Journal, 9*(1). https://doi.org/10.25219/epoj.2020.00108.

Case study 7

Glasgow Alliance to End Homelessness (2020–2023)

This alliance used a city-wide approach to provide support and services for those who were homeless or at risk of homelessness in Glasgow, Scotland – such as accommodation, personal support and routes into employment. Its objectives included: ending rough sleeping; preventing and alleviating the impacts of homelessness; reducing the length of time people spent in temporary accommodation; minimising repeat homelessness; and helping people who were formerly homeless maintain their tenancies.

Alongside the Glasgow Health and Social Care Partnership, seven provider organisations made up the Alliance, which was contracted to run for seven years with an annual budget of around £23 million.

Creating the Alliance

Glasgow's Health and Social Care Partnership was keen to explore collaboration across the city for homelessness services rather than maintain the existing piecemeal approach. Alliance contracting seemed to be a good fit, and it had strong senior-level support for proceeding.

Glasgow Homeless Network (now Homeless Network Scotland) had provided a collaborative space for providers and people with lived experiences to come together. There had been a co-produced, city-wide review of homelessness services, where the need for a more collaborative way of working was established. This was followed in 2017 by a series of workshops to co-design outcomes and shape the emerging ideas. The Health and Social Care Partnership was able to take these forward into the specification.

Glasgow Homeless Network also created a team of people with lived experiences to help with the evaluation of bids during open-market procurement and with continued expert advice to the Alliance. The procurement in 2019 used a competitive dialogue procedure, with the preferred bidding group announced towards the end of the year and the Alliance launching in April 2020.

Progress of the Alliance

The Alliance went live just as the coronavirus pandemic started, which had a considerable impact. There was no opportunity for Alliance members to meet face to face for the first 12–18 months. Launch workshops, so important after the uncertainty and competitive nature of their procurement, were cancelled and regular Shadow and then full Alliance Leadership Team meetings were held virtually. Those in alliance member organisations who would be working together could not meet in person.

The negative impact of the pandemic was compounded by changes in the ALT. Those in senior positions in the provider organisations had built high levels of trust and collaboration throughout the procurement, meeting weekly for a morning for over one year. Unfortunately, several key personnel left their roles (and therefore the Alliance) after its launch. The Glasgow Health and Social Care Partnership representatives also underwent changes. As a result the ALT had to form and reform itself a number of times.

In addition, there was a two-stage approach to moving from existing contracts to the Alliance Agreement. For the first two years the Health and Social Care Partnership continued on existing contracts with provider members while providing start-up funding for collaborative activities and the overarching alliance. It planned to move to a full alliance after the first two years once a new service design with a set of delivery, finance and other plans was approved.

Not surprisingly, given the pandemic, the mixed arrangements and the changes of personnel, it was difficult to establish the alliance way of working. Despite the good will, high levels of commitment and strong desire to make the Alliance work, it was mutually agreed to terminate it in the autumn of 2023.

7   Alliance relationships

Alliances do not exist in a vacuum, and relationships with those outside the alliance have a big impact on its success. It is highly likely that the alliance will not be able to meet its aims and objectives without help, support or permission from those around it. In addition, your alliance will be impacted by the economic and political environment, both local and national. While much of this will be beyond your control, there are insights from alliances that might be helpful.

Each alliance is unique and will have different stakeholders. Here we look at the main groups, with examples from alliances that are up and running. At the end of the chapter you will be able to describe your main external stakeholders and how to develop strong relationships with them.

People with lived experience

In recent years the benefits of co-producing services with the people who use them has been increasingly recognised. Not only is it the right thing to do, but co-production also leads to services that are more likely to be used well, effectively and efficiently.

I learnt a lot about co-production from the early pioneers of alliance contracting in health and care, such as Denis O'Rourke and Nick Dixon, whom I met through a joint initiative between the UK Cabinet Office and Nesta (the UK's innovation agency for social good) called People Powered Health. This was all about putting people front and centre in creating health and wellbeing. It seems that openness to those with lived experiences goes hand in hand with openness to use collaborative commissioning and contracting.

This is also evident when working with colleagues at the Ideas Alliance CIC, a consultancy specialising in co-production. We work with local authorities on co-designing projects with communities, and inevitably get to a point where a council wants to put the great ideas into practice. There is recognition that doing this by commissioning in the usual way will not work and that other collaborative methods are needed. This often results in alliance contracting as

DOI: 10.4324/9781003511809-7

an option. The common values and principles in co-production and alliancing go hand in hand.

Co-production in alliances

Co-design of the Alliance Mandate

It is now unusual to find a local authority who has developed a new service or redesigned an existing one without talking with local people and those with lived experience. They have valuable insights and see aspects of a service that no one else could.

An Alliance Mandate that has been created by or with the people it is being set up for will have a validity that cannot be questioned. The next step is to make sure that those elements that have been strongly stated are kept alive and prominent throughout. In an early alliance, I was present at a two-day event to capture people's experiences related to mental health, and one of their strongest pleas was for respect – to be respected, listened to, heard and understood. I remember this being summarised as 'The way your GP (local doctor) respects and listens to you on that first visit makes all the difference to everything that follows.

How do you capture that in a mandate? How do you keep it alive and prominent in everyone's mind in your alliance?

Fortunately, almost everyone I met in that alliance were people who inherently understood those issues. We were careful with the language we used in anything related to the alliance and kept style of delivery, including respect, as one of the handful of outcomes.

Selection of alliance members

People with lived experiences are often on evaluation panels for the procurement of services as their perspectives and insights will differ from those of others, adding to the range of perspectives that help ensure the right bidders are selected. With the caveat that it ended early, the Glasgow Alliance is a good example of investment in co-production.

Alliance in practice – Glasgow Alliance to End Homelessness

Glasgow has a team of people with lived experience of homelessness called the Glasgow Homelessness Involvement & Feedback Team (GHIFT). It is hosted by Homeless Network Scotland, previously the

Glasgow Homeless Network, an organisation independent of providers or commissioners. Members of the team are available to provide insights and advice on any matter related to homelessness. Glasgow City Council benefitted from their expertise as it developed the mandate for the Glasgow Alliance to End Homelessness.

When it came to the procurement phase, Glasgow City Council knew it wanted the strong voice of people with lived experiences, so it funded the Homeless Network to train some GHIFT members to be evaluators. Ten people in total attended eight all-day training sessions covering specifics about the planned Glasgow Alliance, alliancing and alliance contracting in general and procurement matters (such as transparency, fairness and objective scoring). We also provided training on observation scoring of scenario workshops that were part of the selection process.

At the end of the training, people were able to take part in the written evaluation of bids, observation and interview sessions. Their insights and perspectives were invaluable. For the scenario workshops, three of the seven evaluators were people with lived experiences.

The Glasgow example shows that investment in people through training and support can take you beyond the tokenism of bringing one person on to an evaluation panel late on. Their contribution in this example was stronger and in greater depth than in other procurements I have witnessed.

Governance and decision making

It is usual to have people with lived experiences as associate members of the Alliance Leadership Team (ALT). As discussed in Chapter 5 on alliance governance, there are different perspectives on this mode of representation. Here we give examples where the alliance is able to work with existing groups and forums.

Alliance in practice – Future Pathways

Future Pathways is an alliance for adult survivors of in-care abuse in Scotland. Before its launch, a series of consultations were held with survivors to determine the types of service required, and their involvement has continued in a number of ways during its operation. For example, people with lived experience are represented on the ALT, and there are engagement events and independently led consultations. The Scottish Government also recently established a 'Voices for a Better Future' group to influence policy and other initiatives, as well as the Alliance's work. The Alliance Leadership Team can consult the group and check that decisions are in line with people's needs and interests.

Future Pathways recognises the value of investment in these arrangements. The Alliance Manager and others make sure that there is a safe, welcoming and trustworthy environment in meetings and events. The wellbeing of everyone in the room is a core value, and they are mindful that adjustment and additional support may be needed to facilitate full participation, in light of past traumatic experiences with professionals.

Alliance in practice – Camden Mental Health Resilience Alliance

Here, a separately funded project has allowed the Camden Alliance to put people at the heart at every level. A group of five people with lived experiences of mental health issues was recruited. They meet frequently and have the support of a dedicated co-ordinator. One of their first tasks was to choose a name and they settled on 'Lived Experience Advisers' (usually shortened to 'LExAs'). They sit on the main teams (two on the ALT and three on the AMT) and contribute to other alliance committees and groups. Their role also involves helping others get involved.

There is a lot of appreciation of what the LExAs bring, including their ability to spot gaps in services based on their own experiences. Their independence is valued, and it is understood that they don't necessarily speak with one voice. They may say different things, which is both acceptable and desirable.

The structured nature of the set-up and the co-ordinator role need resources of course, but the benefits are clear to see. It moves co-production beyond tokenism and puts people with lived experience alongside everyone else as equals.

Support and services

As alliances are often developed in places where there is a strong ethos of co-production, there are lots of examples of people's involvement in delivery. They range from specific support, including dedicated phone support for people experiencing mental health crisis in Lambeth, through to a user-led organisation being a member of the Cardiff and Vale Alliance (see Case Study 10).

Evaluating an alliance

Progress in achieving the outcomes of an alliance will usually involve some form of feedback from people using its services. Typically, there will be individual outcomes, with the Well-being Star or the Warwick-Edinburgh Mental Wellbeing Scales (WEMWBS) commonly used.

The outcomes that relate to relationships and interactions, such as those about respect and trust, may require additional and bespoke methods. These need not be questionnaires; they might include stories or focus group interviews, whether at the time of contact or much later. The method used needs to be appropriate and relevant to the context.

In alliances that include well-run groups of people with lived experiences, they can have a range of roles in evaluation – from organising wider feedback through to being arbiters of progress overall. For example, in one alliance we were close to having an evaluation panel made up of people who used its services. The idea was that they would be presented with all the information about progress on outcomes and could decide whether the alliance had made sufficient progress in a particular year.

Of course, if their judgement led to the release of gainshare funds or the payment of painshare, issues of impartiality and conflicts of interest would need attention. However this would be no different to involving people in awarding contracts and other decisions with financial implications.

That initiative didn't come to pass, but maybe something similar will in a future alliance.

Other providers of support and services

It is unlikely that the members of an alliance will be the only providers of services and support in its area of operation. For example, multiple people and organisations contribute to mental health, homelessness and other services. Many will be unfunded, including families and informal support; but some will receive funding from the local authority or commissioner members of the alliance, while others will receive charitable and other funds.

Other people and organisations are therefore important to the alliance, and vice versa. There will be commonality with the aims of the alliance and, usually, shared values. Alliances are part of an ecosystem and will be cognisant of their place in it. An alliance may create resentment, especially when other organisations put together bids to join it and were unsuccessful. Or it may be that the alliance members are seen as 'the chosen ones' with seats around the high table with high funding levels and profile. Others can feel excluded and less important. For example, in one of our alliances, someone who had been there since the beginning said: 'We were seen as the destroyer, it was very difficult. We were blamed for the actions the council had taken'; and in another they talked about feeling 'sabotaged' by the actions of those who had been part of a losing bid.

Over time, these perceptions and sentiments fade, especially if the alliance is seen to be effective and inclusive. Here is an example of how one alliance approached its role.

Alliance in practice – Lambeth Living Well Network Alliance

The Alliance operates within the Lambeth Living Well Network, making a connection between the Alliance and the much wider network of those providing and invested in mental health services. The Alliance arranges regular meetings and events with anyone interested in mental health in the borough. The LLW Network provides the Alliance with insights and ideas, and these mutual benefits mean there are good relationships and connections.

As well as organising get-togethers with partners, an alliance will be asked to attend other groups, committees and working parties. It will be seen as a key player, so these invitations can be numerous. On the one hand, as someone said to me of one alliance, at least we only have to invite the alliance, not each member separately. On the other hand, those in the alliance will need to share the workload and trust each other to represent its views.

Communities

During the time we have established alliancing in the UK public sector there has been a growing awareness of the power of communities. Movements such as Asset Based Community Development (ABCD), spearheaded by Cormac Russell, champion communities 'doing it for themselves'

(Russell & McKnight, 2022). For them, institutions and services that aim to 'help' are actually doing the opposite by inhibiting or ignoring the everyday interactions that take place in every community. Another example is Community Catalysts, a collective that builds on the strength of people and communities to enable microenterprises to support and care for other local people.

For those in these circles, the language of 'services' and 'people using services' is felt to be archaic and paternalistic. Even the best-meaning and most co-productive local charity might still fall into doing 'to' and 'for' rather than doing 'with'. This is especially so if there is external funding; and, the larger the amount of public funding, the more desire there is for reporting and accountability processes.

I am aware that alliancing is a tool for buying and managing services. While we are careful about language and try to keep a focus on people rather than services, we cannot get away from the fact that this is about how public money is used to create the kind of support and services that other movements see as problematic.

For me, the challenge is how to develop funding and accountability methods that support people-led support and collaboration. I believe this presents an opportunity. It would be amazing to see how the principles of alliancing and true collaboration can meet with the values and experiences of the people, communities and community-led enterprises to create a powerful way to harness public money in a devolved and well-distributed manner.

While most alliances have good connections to their local communities, we are still at an early stage of building community-led alliances. As our experience and learning of commissioner-mandated alliances grows, there is potential to explore further adaptations to the collaborative model to harness the power of communities.

Political and economic environment

Looking back to 2012, I sometimes think we could not have chosen a more difficult time to try out an innovation in the UK public sector. The financial impact of austerity greatly affected public sector funding, and Brexit led to further upheavals and uncertainties, especially around recruitment.

On the one hand there has been the impetus to try something new, the burning platform that required new thinking and action. On the other, it has meant that those working in public service or in charities and social enterprises that are dependent on public monies (fully or in part) are continuously under pressure.

Then came the pandemic and the cost of living crisis, which increased demand in all alliances, whether for homelessness, wellbeing or mental health support. The numbers of people making contact for support and services have rocketed.

Of course, this can encourage further creativity and be a positive force for change. As more people become familiar with interactions online and technology improves, virtual points of access and online support become easier. This allowed alliances to connect with people during the lockdowns of 2020 and 2021, and virtual contact is now normal everywhere.

However, there is no getting away from the difficulties. To be innovative, you need people to have headroom to think and to experiment. That is almost impossible when you are permanently understaffed, stressed, fire-fighting and exhausted. People need to be able to try things that don't work out; people need to be allowed to fail. Again, this is difficult in organisations under pressure and scrutiny.

Alliances thrive when relationships between people are good – between member organisations, their representatives and leaders, and the people who work in them as they work alongside others. Building those strong relationships early in an alliance's life will give it the resilience needed to face adversity and challenges later on. The longer-established alliances have got through the pandemic years well, albeit with challenges and the need to adapt.

Alliance in practice – The Plymouth Alliance

The Plymouth Alliance went live in 2019 and had a very good first year. The decision had been made to give it responsibility for the bed and breakfast (B&B) budget in the city, which, historically, was exceeded every year with more people in emergency accommodation than planned. In that first year, by working together and focusing on avoidance, the budget was underspent.

Then Covid hit, followed by the impact of inflation and the cost of living crisis, leading to massively increased demand. The emergency accommodation budget was again under considerable pressure. The significant increases in B&B costs meant that this part of the budget was leading to financial difficulties for the Alliance. As there were small organisations alongside larger ones, their ability to handle financial risk differed.

The Plymouth Alliance worked through the crisis, helped considerably by the council taking back responsibility for the emergency accommodation costs. However, Alliance members still work together to support that agenda.

As well as demand and the financial impacts of political and economic decisions, there are also organisational changes that can affect alliances.

Alliance in practice – The Lambeth Alliances

When the Lambeth Alliances were being set up in 2013–2018, one of the commissioners was the then Lambeth Clinical Commissioning Group. Decisions on health care spending were at borough level, making it easy to work with Lambeth Council on joint initiatives.

Health commissioning moved to the regional level with the eventual creation of NHS South East London Integrated Care Board. On paper, therefore, the link with Lambeth only relates to one part of the South East London health system. This could have led to reduced commitment from NHS commissioners or even dissolution of the Alliance. Fortunately, the Commissioner as Owner role in the previous arrangement was the Director of Finance who took up the regional role. Her personal interest and commitment has allowed continuity for all, and the Alliance was mostly shielded from the wider organisational upheaval.

Summary

Alliances do not exist in isolation. The relationships around them are pivotal to their success and even survival. Public sector organisations and funding are always subject to the politics and economic decisions of the current government. People with lived experiences and those who use services can help, guide and advise at every stage of an alliance, from mandate development and selection of members, to the design and delivery of services and evaluation.

Most alliances bring together people who already have strong networks and longstanding ties with other people and organisations who share their aims and objectives. Working with them on behalf of the alliance to help achieve those aims is a fundamental task for all involved.

In the final chapter we look at how alliances evolve over time, going through different stages as the months and years go by.

Reference

Russell, C., & McKnight, J. (2022). *The connected community: Discovering the health, wealth, and power of neighborhoods.* Berrett-Koehler.

Case study 8

County Durham Mental Health and Wellbeing Alliance (2022–present)

This alliance provides a range of support services for mental health wellbeing, including prevention, early identification and recovery support. It was set up by Durham County Council with County Durham Care Partnership and seven voluntary and community sector organisations. Annual funding started at £2.3 million, and the contract is for seven years with an option to extend for a further three.

Creating the Alliance

Durham County Council chose alliance contracting as it would bring a unified set of services with collaboration between providers and improve access to 21 separate services. It held an open market procurement process in the summer of 2021, and, once the preferred bidding group was confirmed, a Shadow Alliance operated for several months prior to the formal launch in April 2022.

Progress of the Alliance

The Alliance set up a single point of access for people looking for help around their mental wellbeing, with referrals taking place either by telephone or via their website. Soon after launch, additional funding from the NHS was secured to extend the scope to provide the first point of contact for GPs and other professionals. Once their needs are assessed, people are introduced to the most appropriate teams across a wide range of free mental health and recovery services, including those that help with relationships, bereavement and suicide. The service also provides support with accommodation, education and employability, as well as physical activity, befriending, finances and more.

Alliance members come together to share information, improve pathways and look at specific issues such as accommodation and outreach. There are several subcontractors that receive funding from the Alliance and a dedicated member of the team links with them, for example in sharing bids and grant opportunities.

The first two years of the Alliance saw an increase in demand and challenging financial context, and it is now looking to make changes to working arrangements as it moves into the next phase. For Julie

Cane (the Alliance Manager) and Tricia Reed (the Durham Council representative on the Alliance Leadership Team) this represents the lifecycle of their alliance: 'It took us 18 months to 2 years to get established and now we are into the hard work of making changes.' They talk about being bold and brave. If the expectation of change is made clear from the outset it is easier to move away from carrying on with no changes year on year. It is recognised that everyone has to be really committed to the aims and purposes, and not just involved in the alliance to secure their own funding.

This alliance has a large number of members. While this allows a good wide range of perspectives, it also means more communication and checking on shared decision making. Those involved recognise the need to continually invest in building and maintaining relationships throughout the lifetime of the alliance.

What changed for people

People in County Durham now have a simplified way of finding support and a wide range of options, with dedicated referral co-ordinators to help them navigate and find the right options. In the first two years, over 6,000 people accessed the service, and there are numerous individual stories of the difference the support they received has made.

For further information see: https://www.durhammentalwellbeingalliance.org.

8　Alliance lifecycle

All alliances go through different stages and, while each alliance is unique, we have observed some similarities. Alliances create a lot of excitement and interest: there is the early set-up and launch when everything is new; people are full of enthusiasm, interest and ideas. Following this, life settles down and some of the underlying issues that may need to be tackled become more obvious. This can be quite a difficult time as it usually coincides with energy flagging. Fortunately most alliances come through this, and you reach a stage where you are really motoring and the full value of being an alliance materialises.

The time to move through each stage will be different for each alliance, and some stages may run concurrently. There is no exact blueprint that everyone follows. To be successful, the alliance will need different focuses and activities at different times. The key is to keep the purpose and vision front and centre at all stages and adhere to the principles and values.

In this chapter I will explain these stages and point out some of the common challenges and how to prevent issues that may lead to the breakdown of trust and relationships. While some of this will be a recap of points already made, we will use the experience of those involved in alliances to bring to life the realities and common issues and problems. In addition, we will look at research undertaken on successful alliances and how to maximise the conditions and opportunities for success. At the end of the chapter you will know what to expect at different times in the life cycle of your alliance and have some tips and ideas for making the most of each stage.

The early months

The time leading up to the launch of an alliance and the early months are periods of intense activity. After all the dreaming and talking about what might be possible, it is time to turn that into reality. The alliance is now real. The novelty and excitement about being part of an innovative and groundbreaking initiative helps maintain energy and enthusiasm. Yet the transition is full

DOI: 10.4324/9781003511809-8

of challenges. There is a lot to do and, typically, all the people or resources needed to do it are not yet in place.

Before an alliance launches there will have been many months and even years of planning and activity. The emotional and time investment by some key people will be huge. There will be high levels of expectation. This expectation extends to everyone who has heard about the alliance, including people using the existing services and support. They will have their own hopes and fears about the change. In the early months of an alliance the weight of expectation, coupled with the enormous list of things to do, can be overwhelming. This is normal and will pass. Here are a few tips to help, some of which we have already covered but I am bringing into one place.

Start planning early

Moving from an idea and a promise of change to the reality of making those happen will start before the actual launch of the alliance. The more that can be done in the pre-alliance phase, the better. This is why we advocate using any procurement process to develop the plans that will be the actual ones for the alliance. Once the procurement process is over, the delivery, workforce, communications and other plans are already created. There may be some tweaks of course, but you are not starting from scratch.

Identify an Alliance Manager and core team

In order to move from planning to implementation, you need people to make that happen. An Alliance Manger, even if interim to start with, is essential. They, in turn, will need one or two people to help.

Set up shadow governance as soon as possible

As discussed in Chapter 3, use the earliest opportunity to get the alliance governance in place. Shadow governance arrangements, beginning well before the start date for the alliance, will give everyone a chance to get used to their new roles and how they interact with each other. When the alliance launches formally, the key people will already have been meeting and working through all the issues.

It is also important to sort out the governance and relationships within member organisations to ensure the alliance has the authority and space to function. As personnel from one alliance said, it took time to sort the governance to be able to keep their individual organisations at arm's length.

Develop report templates

Even though it is hard to collect and collate information when there are disparate systems and teams and no one is yet used to the new approach, it is advisable to get into the routine of reporting cycles. The longer there is a delay with no sense of what the alliance is achieving, the more frustration will build.

We suggest you develop a report template based on the outcomes and objectives and start using it even if there are a lot of blank sections initially. It will focus attention on what is needed to get the required data or insights. As time progresses, the reports will become more populated and you can see the progress you are making.

Manage expectations about pace of change

Different expectations of how quickly you can move can be a precursor to breakdown of trust and relationships, especially if one or more people or organisations are seen as holding others back. People with lived experience and those who use existing services will have heard about impending changes and the improvements they will bring. It is then disappointing if it feels as if nothing has changed.

Providers had the euphoria of winning the bid after months of putting new ideas into a tender process. Now reality kicks in and it can feel harder than they had envisaged. Commissioners have led the project, maybe over one or two years. They finally have the alliance in place, and three months later everyone is bogged down in sorting out micro-level issues. With all the heightened expectations, people may express frustration, and the atmosphere in meetings becomes heated.

There is no easy answer to this as you want the pressure to make changes to be there, but too much can become unhelpful. It is therefore important to be able to discuss issues in a non-threatening and non-emotional way. The Alliance Manager is key here. It will help them to have timelines that are both aspirational and realistic and that they have the capacity around them to meet those milestones. The role of the Alliance Leadership Team (ALT) in preventing or removing obstacles to progress will be important.

Communicate often and widely

Your list of stakeholders will be long, but the more you can listen to them, update them and talk to them the better. You will, of course, need to prioritise and be realistic about what you can do. A nominated communications lead to help you co-ordinate this should be an early consideration.

Create space for reflection and development

While there are many practicalities and tasks to consider, it is just as important to check in about how things feel and how you are working to the alliance principles. This can be done in a few minutes at the end of meetings, asking everyone to say how it is feeling to them. It is also useful to have an observer at meetings who can feed back about interactions and process.

A programme of individual and team coaching for key personnel will be highly beneficial. Even the most experienced leaders and managers will need a period of adjustment in their new roles, and space and time to reflect will be welcome.

We often get requests for help with group dynamics, especially around difficult conversations. If you can get advice and facilitation for these in advance, it can be much better than waiting until tensions have arisen and trust is starting to fall.

Settling down

After the first 6–9 months you will find that things slowly start to settle down. It could be longer though, and some alliances may take about 18 months or even two years to do so. However long it takes, you will get to a point where your alliance is established, becoming well known and starting to make a difference. Hopefully by now you have key personnel in post and overall leadership and management structures that are working well. You should enjoy this quieter time, but don't be complacent. Now is a good time to review your progress and make adjustments based on the feedback.

Health check

We recommend a full day where all members of the Alliance Leadership Team can take time to look back at what has been achieved and consider whether there are any gaps or changes to make. By now, you will have become set in how you do things, and may not have realised or addressed areas where you can be more effective or inclusive.

When I have done this, I have advised that we keep the focus on how you are keeping the vision and purpose front and centre and applying the alliance principles and your alliance's values. You can score each principle on how evident it is in how you are working together. This always generates interesting conversations and, not infrequently, a divergence of views. I like to build on the positives, for instance, how you have managed something difficult well and what made that a good experience. This is preferable to dwelling on times when it did not feel so good. Of course, you cannot ignore any bad feelings, and there may be important areas of conflict that need to be addressed. It is about balance as we all tend to let one or two bad incidents block out the many more good ones.

In some places the day has been just for the Alliance Leadership Team and Alliance Manager, while in others we included the Alliance Management Team (AMT) for some or all of the time. It is up to you. The important thing is to book a day in the diary and use it to celebrate all you have achieved to date and to share ideas about how you will work even better going forward.

Voices of experience

To help give a sense of the reality, we can draw on the reflections of those who are involved in alliances. Since 2020 there have been six weekly video meetings with Alliance Managers and, separately, commissioners. These are open discussions where anyone can raise issues they want to discuss. Colleagues help each other with insights and advice, or just listen and offer support. After each meeting, I summarise the main themes in an email. This has created a log of the real issues facing people who are at the core of alliances. Below is a summary of common recurring themes as pointers to where you might want to invest time and energy.

Alliance manager themes

Core team/infrastructure

The topic the managers raised most frequently concerned the core team – or rather the lack of a core team. The Alliance Manager's role is a difficult one at the best of times, and having no administrative support compounds that. When a new manager joined the group, others would give advice based on a list of 'what I wish I had known or done when I started'. Appointing a core team was always on that list, with administration, communications and data and finance analysts most cited.

Finance and risk sharing

In the next commonest topics people mentioned discussions and decisions about financial issues being the most challenging for their alliance. In the group, discussions covered lots of aspects of good advance planning and reporting cycles. There were highly specific questions about salary levels and who funds what, through to the strategic dimensions of trying to achieve equitability and setting expectations of change rather than just rolling over everyone's allocation.

Governance and the ALT

The role of the ALT, AMT and commissioners were frequent topics of conversation. For Alliance Managers, a properly functioning ALT was pivotal; or rather, a less than properly functioning ALT was problematic. In different alliances there were periods of ALTs being overreaching and not leaving the manager room for discretion and freedom to act. Another common complaint was of ALTs not making timely decisions, with Alliance Managers feeling they had to spend a lot of time 'managing up' in order to be able to function.

On the positive side, some Alliance Managers had a good relationship and dynamic with their ALT. They were able to talk about what they had done or continued to do from their side to maintain that relationship, and we often reflected on what was it about their ALTs that made a difference. There was no single element, but clarity of roles, individuals who understand good governance and willingness to trust and stand back were often cited.

Planning, performance and reporting

The operational management elements of the Alliance Manager's role were often shared at the meetings, with people comparing amounts, frequency and methods used. Undertaking these functions across a number of organisations poses challenges, and there were a range of levels of detail and rigour among the alliances.

Other issues

The many other topics of conversation included culture, workforce, procurement and subcontractors, scope creep, relationships with partners and demand management, to name a few.

Alliance commissioner themes

Changes to ALT membership

As noted before, people leaving and new people joining an alliance need to be managed well. As alliancing is a relatively new way of working, people are unlikely to have prior experience of or be familiar with the principles and alliance ways of working. Commissioners talk about taking time to induct and support new members into the team so they can be clear on expectations and be effective in their new roles.

The Alliance Manager role

The importance and qualities of Alliance Managers and, for some, Alliance Directors were other frequent topics of discussion. People talked about the importance of a full and open recruitment process, clarity and choice of management and support for the Alliance Manager, and how to avoid conflicts of interest. Different alliances have taken different approaches to the role, including appointing a third party to host them.

Another challenge that sometimes arises is that, as the alliance develops and people see it is delivering and making change happen, the Alliance Manager is asked to get involved with more transformational activity outside of the alliance. This can divert focus and resources from the alliance and affect its performance.

Growing the alliance

Another common theme is that, as the alliance evolves and starts to deliver change, it develops a reputation for being a place that makes things happen and gets things done. While this is positive, the risk is that others want the alliance to take on new and different responsibilities before it has had chance to establish itself and embed. It can be tricky to balance this with growing the alliance in a sustainable way.

Managing conflict and difficult conversations

As with any leadership team, differences and conflict will arise at times, and people shared their experiences of this. They talked about how to have transparent and honest conversations about difficult issues in a way that keeps the alliance together. It helps to remember that differences can be also positive, and often generate the most creative ideas when managed well. Remaining focused on the common purpose and principles that everyone has signed up to is also key to working through difficulties when they arise.

Open-book accounting

Once alliances have got through the initial stage of development, they will often turn their attention to the principle of open-book accounting. For some, this revealed that people didn't really understand what it means and how to work well with it. They talked about the importance of spending time together, working through what open-book accounting is, why it is important and how you can do it in a practical way.

Alliance contracts ending

For more established alliances, as their contracts neared the end, commissioners found themselves needing to make the case for renewing the contract. Although they had a range of evidence to draw on to demonstrate the impact of the alliance, they also found they needed to manage expectations. Alliances do not fix everything, and sometimes there are unrealistic expectations about what others expect from an alliance.

The motoring phase

One Alliance Manager described this stage well, saying it felt as if the hard graft of the early years of her alliance was now paying off and it was into innovation and genuine transformation. By now the alliance will be well established and firmly part of everyday working. Those involved will be experienced collaborators and team players. Shared decision making and joint responsibility will be nothing new.

Successful alliances will already have made significant progress and will be challenging themselves to go even further. They will be creating new ways of supporting people and working together for the benefit of all. There will be data and stories that show the difference the alliance is making.

So what makes a successful alliance?

When I started talking with people about alliancing, they commonly asked about published evidence that they work. Not surprisingly, there are no randomly controlled trials that can show this definitively. Alliances exist in context-specific, complex environments. No two alliances are the same, and nor are the circumstances in which they are set up.

I realised there was a different question to ask. It was about what makes an alliance successful. While I found a lot of publications on alliances, it was hard to find consistency or anything that drew together key findings. The solution was to do the analysis myself. I was lucky enough to be working with a fantastic colleague, Nadine Spalburg. She took the project on, undertaking a literature search and meticulously analysing the findings to identify themes. The results were presented at the 2016 International Conference for Integrated Care in Barcelona (Spain) and the abstract published in the *International Journal for Integrated Care* (Hutchinson & Spalburg, 2016).

We identified over 80 publications that fitted our criteria of being about alliances and having some element of description of success. They covered a wide range of basic research, observational studies and theoretical frameworks. The areas involved included manufacturing, biotechnology, construction, the public sector, service industries and pharmaceuticals. It was fascinating that 'success' was defined in numerous ways. There was no one way to ask 'Did it work?' Different dimensions of success included those based on economics, performance outcomes achieved, resources, competence, relationships or competitive advantage. Despite this diversity, the following clear themes emerged:

- trust and loyalty between parties
- high-quality decision-making processes
- alliance management capability and skills
- flexibility and dynamism.

The evidence base for successful alliances – executive summary

A literature review was undertaken to determine the evidence base for successful alliancing. Alliancing and alliance contracting are generating interest as tools for driving collaboration and integrated working in health and other public services. It is important to understand what makes alliances successful so that we can incorporate the learning and experience of others as we apply them in new contexts.

We conducted searches in Google Scholar for variations of the terms 'alliance' and 'alliance contracts'. Further material came from reference lists in relevant papers and requests to alliance specialists. Over 80 publications were identified, covering a wide range and depth of basic research, observational studies and theoretical frameworks. Our analysis showed that:

1. Alliances are flexible and adaptable, so can take many forms. The well-described 'project alliances', typically in infrastructure and construction, are one subset, and industry strategic alliances for mutual benefit in the market are another. In between are numerous hybrid forms that are created for particular circumstances.
2. Alliance success is also broadly defined. Traditional economic measures and achievement of objectives are commonly seen as the core elements, but other benefits are also described. These can be the synergy of bringing resources together, creation of new skills and capabilities, durable relationships and competitive advantage.

Taking the above into account, it is hard to aggregate the literature to quantify the impact of any single factor on success. However our analysis shows that, regardless of the type of alliance or the sector or industry, the same following interrelated and interdependent themes emerge:

a. Trust and loyalty between parties

Trust substitutes for hierarchical control. Partner selection and strategic, goal and incentive congruence are critical. Uncertainty about partner behaviour hinders the establishment of trust. Reducing the risk of partner opportunism requires attention to differences in economic benefits, cultural diversity and the time horizon for return on the investment for each partner. Interestingly equity alliances (where there is a shared investment between parties) appear to engender stronger partner loyalty and are more successful than non-equity alliances.

b. High-quality decision-making processes

Alliances create a unique context for decision making with unanimity and participatory processes. Appropriate governance arrangements are needed but not enough. There has to be trust and reciprocity between partners as well as the ability to employ and flex various ways to co-ordinate interactions and activities as the alliance evolves over time. Constraints on high quality decision-making are multiple decision making centres, uncertainty about partners, ambiguity about the evolution of the alliance and political and micropolitical actions.

c. Alliance management capability and skills

The multiparty context of alliances requires considerable management capability. Three distinct skills are co-ordination of joint tasks, communication with sharing of relevant knowledge and information and a bonding process for social integration. Proactiveness and ability to modify the alliance activities over time are positive aspects. All these are self-reinforcing, building management effectiveness as experience grows. Challenges arise when there are divided authority structures, information asymmetries and underdeveloped personal relationships.

d. Flexibility and dynamism

Although woven into the other three themes, flexibility and dynamism stand out as themes in their own right. Alliances are, by design, flexible and must evolve to accommodate contextual changes. The co-ordination, social norms, planning and capabilities must all reflect this, and the leadership and management need to be able to function with ambiguity and uncertainty.

Hutchinson & Spalburg (2016).

Since we undertook the literature review, all my experience has reconfirmed these findings. High levels of trust, good governance, strong management capabilities and flexibility are essential requirements for a successful alliance. With them, there will still be difficult times; without them, it will be impossible.

The way you define success for your alliance will be individual to you and your context. However, the four themes identified above will apply to all alliances. They provide a framework for checking that your alliance is able to maximise the opportunities it has. The following is a suggestion for generating discussion and action points based on these themes. It works well as part of a strategy awayday or other review and planning day.

Workshop exercise – themes for successful alliances

After introducing the four themes – trust and loyalty between parties, high-quality decision making, alliance management capability and skills, and flexibility and dynamism – arrange people into groups.

- Provide scoring sheets with a scale of 'excellent, good, fair, could be better' for each theme. Leave space for people to write examples of why they have chosen a particular score.
- Ask everyone to complete their scores individually, and then ask them to discuss in small groups what they have written and thought about. What are the similarities? Are there any differences in how people see and experience the alliance? The conversations will generate important insights and ideas. Have someone note these down ready for whole room feedback.
- Ask each group to come up with ideas for how you can do even better on the four themes. You can talk about what a realistic score might be and what that would entail.
- Have a whole room session to collate all the ideas and devise a plan of action.

End of an alliance

I was once told that the success of an alliance is not about its longevity. How long an alliance operates for should not be linked to success. The external environment is constantly changing, and there may be good reasons to move to a different model or a different alliance with time.

Even the most successful alliances will have an end of contract date. Usually there is a rollover and more years added, but, eventually, the alliance will be expected to end. Planning for closure therefore needs to start well in advance, two to three years even. As with large change projects or other closures, numerous activities are needed, including calculation of exit costs, data storage, care of workforce, communications and legacy.

Summary

No alliance stands still. All will go through different phases where energy and enthusiasm levels, pace of change and sense of momentum will vary. While there are no easy answers to keep your alliance functioning on tip-top form every day, there are some areas to focus on and some learning from others who have been there before.

The early months of an alliance is a period of intense activity and change, and can feel completely overwhelming. This is normal and it will pass. Attention to the basics of governance, roles, relationships and trust-building will help mitigate the potential for frustrations to escalate.

Once the initial flurry of activity in the early life of the alliance abates, you will have an opportunity to reflect on where you are doing well and whether there are any gaps. Now is a good time to make any tweaks to governance, ways of working and management and reporting. This will stand you in good stead for the acceleration of change to come. There is plenty of experience from alliances already in action as well as independent facilitators who can give objective support. Tapping into these will show you are not alone.

Once you are well into the second year of an alliance it should feel like business as usual, the normal way of working. You will be seeing the impacts for people and are able to reap the benefits of being an alliance. You can celebrate your achievements and review whether there is more you can do to make a difference.

Reference

Hutchinson, L., & Spalburg, N. (2016). The evidence base for successful alliancing. *International Journal of Integrated Care*, *16*(6), A122. https://doi.org/10.5334/ijic.2670.

Case study 9

The Camden Mental Health Resilience Alliance (2022–present)

This alliance coordinates and manages a range of support and services for people in the London borough of Camden who are concerned about their own mental wellbeing or that of family or friends. It builds on the Mental Health Resilience Network, a borough-wide network of voluntary and community providers of support and services. Camden Council wanted to move to the next level of collaboration and chose alliance contracting as the vehicle for this.

The Alliance launched in April 2022 after open-market procurement. It includes four provider members and the council. The annual budget is £900,000, and the contract term is two years with one-year extension and the possibility of a longer contract dependent on performance over the first two years.

Creating the Alliance

The Mental Health Resilience Network in Camden had been in place since 2015. During the pandemic, the services that make up the Network had formed a critical contribution to the local Covid-19 response, and effectively adapted their services to respond to residents' needs. Residents had been positive about the Network, but also stated they wanted to see more prevention and more joining up of services. The council therefore decided to move to an alliance contract. Firstly, they confirmed the outcomes and priorities for the Alliance from existing work, and then developed the specification and draft Alliance Agreement. Procurement commenced in October 2021 and was completed the following February.

Progress of the Alliance

The Alliance benefited from a clear vision from the commissioners and providers from the outset. They created a core infrastructure with shared posts and an emphasis on co-production through Lived Experience Advisers. The focus has been on learning and building a culture of true collaboration. Moving to a single point of access took longer than expected and went live two years after the launch. This may, in part, reflect frequent changes of Alliance Managers over that time.

Overall, although individual services have not changed significantly, there is more connection and awareness between members. There is shared reporting and, at the time of writing, plans to further streamline data collection, including reporting on social value. Members of the Alliance also see the impact of the model and experience of joined-up working in other parts of their work.

What changed for people

At the instigation of the Lived Experience Advisers, feedback from people who have accessed support was collected. It shows that the support and services run and co-ordinated by the Alliance are well received: 93 per cent said they have been able to direct and dictate their Alliance support; 93 per cent reported they had achieved what they wanted; and 100 per cent reported being satisfied with the service.

Those who work in the Alliance are also positive, reflecting that they increasingly feel part of a whole, not just of their own organisation. They also report on the sense of collectively helping to build capacity in a complex system.

Case study 10

Cardiff and Vale Drug and Alcohol Service Alliance (2022–present)

This Alliance in Wales was set up to transform and embed change in substance use services for children and adults. It launched in August 2022 after open-market procurement. The provider members are three third sector organisations delivering substance misuse services across the country that came together to deliver services in the Cardiff and Vale region. Annual funding started at £2.5 million over the contract term of ten years, and there were increases in funding for the first three years.

Creating the Alliance

The Cardiff and Vale Area Planning Board were keen to move to a more outcome-based approach to commissioning services. A set of outcomes and service qualities for drug and alcohol services had recently been developed. They also wanted to build in more co-production and collaboration. When the current services for people affected by substance misuse were up for recommissioning, they decided to use an alliance contracting approach.

Using a competitive dialogue process, the procurement commenced in October 2021. As part of the evaluation, scenario workshops to test bidding groups' commitment to collaboration and innovation was used, albeit held online due to ongoing pandemic restrictions. The preferred bidder was announced in April 2022, and shadow arrangements were put in place until the launch in August that year.

Progress of the Alliance

After 20 months in operation, those involved in the Alliance talked about the differences they have experienced between the alliance model and other partnerships: that it has taken a while to really understand it and get the governance clear in their minds and functioning well. More direction and coaching on the model and elements of the governance, specifically the Alliance Manager role, would have been welcome. There was an in-depth needs assessment prior to developing the Alliance, which led to a clear set of outcomes and service qualities. These are highly valued as they provide focus for where to invest time, resources and energy.

This alliance has a ten-year contract, and there is recognition that change takes time and that it is a long-term project. Challenges remain around restrictions due to the government grant system enforcing ring-fencing of some funds. As with all alliances, the connections and relationships with others, for instance criminal justice and health partners, is complex. The initial focus was on foundations: shared purpose; how to achieve it; and creating a 'new normal' with a shared culture and processes from the different member organisations coming together. The leaders are very aware of the importance of strong leadership in driving the collaborative approach and providing clarity for the workforce.

What changed for people

It is still early days and there is much to do. One feature of this alliance is that one of its partners is a member-led organisation. This has given legitimacy to the voice of those with lived experience, recognising and embedding their role in recovery services and valuing what they bring as different and unique.

For more information see: https://www.cavdas.com.

Conclusion

The years since 2012 have been a journey of discovery as we have taken alliancing – a methodology in use in very different contexts – and applied it to health and care. I have tried to put down in this book the main learning from our experiences.

The alliances we have created have been in the UK but within different political, structural and financial systems. The UK will have features that make alliancing easier than in other countries, but the opposite will be true too. The context matters for the detail; but it is desire and commitment that are needed to get started in the first place. That can happen anywhere.

Of course, there are other ways to move from a system based on individual service contracts to one that is open and focused on purpose and relationships. That is a big change to make; and, in my view, alliance contracting has provided an established methodology that allowed the pioneers to persuade their colleagues to take the first step. It has been a catalyst that needs and will always need key ingredients to be able to work. Those ingredients are commitment to collaboration and a shared purpose.

There is no single way to create or run an alliance. Each of the case studies in this volume has its own unique context and features. If there is a commonality, it relates to the alliance principles. I am struck by how many people from the alliances described here still, to this day, talk about 'best for people' and unanimous decision making. Those principles and the values behind them have persisted and survived. Looking back and thinking about the journey each alliance has been on and what factors have helped and what has hindered, there are a few things that stand out.

First is size. When I started out I expected that alliances would be entities with large budgets and a small number of big players as members. The time commitment for all those involved made me think that it would only be worth it for big projects. In fact it was the opposite, with the early alliances providing discrete, focused sets of support and services for relatively small budgets. We now have a range of sizes and, while it can harder for the smaller ones, they seem to be managing well.

DOI: 10.4324/9781003511809-9

Longer contract lengths are beneficial in giving time to embed new ways of working, build trust and then move to change management. Stability and certainty help, and those in the alliances often cite these as key to being able to make an impact. However, those alliances on shorter contracts have found ways to get the most from their collaboration and plan for extended futures.

Two important factors are the stability of the groups involved and the deep understanding of alliancing, especially in commissioning organisations. Of course, one cannot avoid turnover of personnel. Deep-seated awareness of alliancing in an organisation may help mitigate changes by replacing someone in a leadership role with someone who also understands the approach. A high level of turnover, with the leadership group having to form, storm and norm multiple times, will hamper progress.

Alliancing is not a magic bullet, and it certainly isn't easy. The challenges never go away; they just change over the lifetime of the alliance. Developing and maintaining trusted relationships requires continuous active considera-tion. Time and again I hear from people in alliances that, although it is hard and at times very challenging, it is a better way than any other. As someone said, 'Yes it is hard but it's the part of my work I enjoy the most.'

The future

There are many people whose hard work and enthusiasm have contributed to these experiences. Future alliances can build on these, confident that they are not the first.

I have been privileged to meet many dedicated people across the UK. It has been pleasurable, challenging, exciting and occasionally scary. I am very proud of all we have achieved and only wish we could have done more. My colleagues at Ideas Alliance CIC will continue to support people who are keen to work together for the benefit of those they serve. Their exper-tise in community-led developments, coupled with in-depth understanding of alliance contracting, is a powerful mix.

For me, this is the exciting future direction for alliancing. We have been testing out collaborative financial, legal and governance arrangements, all necessary when large amounts of public money are in play. Where possible, we have strengthened co-production and brought the power of lived experi-ence into the mix. However, we are only just at the beginning of melding the formality of public financial governance and reporting with the freedom and openness of truly community- and people-led initiatives.

Maybe in the future we will be able to find a way to bring these together as there are shared underlying principles and intent. That would be an important and powerful next step. Whatever the future direction, one thing is for sure: the desire and need for collaboration will never go away.

Appendix
Alliance Principles

Principle 1 – Collective responsibility

a) To assume collective responsibility for all risks involved in providing services under this Agreement:

- Everyone takes responsibility for the whole rather than just their direct area of focus.
- It means everyone has to understand the whole and people share ideas and perspectives throughout.
- Sharing of understanding and learning about others are rich and rewarding aspects of being a member of an alliance.
- In practice it means that, while each organisation manages the delivery risks of their part of the services, everyone has a role in planning, operation, overall co-ordination and, of course, the Alliance's success or failure.

Principle 2 – Best for people decision making

b) To make decisions on a 'best for people using services' basis:

- All major decisions are made as best for people using services, not on the basis of any member's self-interest. Decisions are not 'best for my organisation'.
- In order for this to work, it is absolutely critical that all alliance members are aligned. Success for the alliance must mean success for each member.
- If there are different views on what is best for people using services, then keep talking. Focus the discussion on people, not member organisations.

Principle 3 – Unanimous decision making

c) To commit to unanimous, principle- and value-based decision making on all key issues:

- Unanimous decisions mean that, whatever the size of the organisation or its financial input into the alliance, everyone will have equal status around the table.
- Being focused on what is best for people should make it easier to come to unanimous agreement.
- Any differences of view need to be heard.
- Unanimous means avoidance of resorting to a majority vote which would mean that there is at least one person who does not think the decision is right, that it is not best for people.
- Unanimous does not mean people use it as a way to veto. Any alliance that starts to think this is the case is an alliance in trouble.
- Unanimous must not mean that people keep quiet if they have misgivings. All views should be heard and considered.
- Unanimous decision making gets harder when you have more members. We advise no more than eight risk-sharing organisations in an alliance.
- The other aspects of this principle are decisions being principle- and value-based. This means the values that the Alliance creates for itself.

Principle 4 – No fault, no blame

d) To adopt a culture of 'no fault, no blame' among Alliance participants, and to seek to avoid all disputes and litigation (except in very limited cases of wilful default):

- This principle is key for innovation.
- Having a no fault, no blame principle is effectively giving people permission to try new things and accepting that not all of them will be successful.
- The focus is on learning from innovation that doesn't work out, not blaming.

Avoidance of disputes

- The dispute process for alliances is deliberately short. The Alliance Management Team is expected to prevent or quickly resolve disputes. If they are unable to then it passes to the Alliance Leadership Team. If they cannot resolve it, the Alliance terminates.

- There is no protracted period of seeking external facilitation or arbitration. An alliance with a dispute requiring these is no longer functioning as an alliance, and therefore should be ended.
- This 'sheer cliff edge' provides a strong incentive to get on top of things quickly, keep talking, and find resolution and compromise as soon as possible.
- No disputes does not mean no disagreements. Differences of opinion, even strong ones, are healthy and a sign of people bringing different perspectives to a discussion. You don't want too much group think developing.

Principle 5 – Open book

e) To adopt open-book accounting and transparency in all matters:

- Everyone has responsibility and accountability for how funds are spent so people will to be able to see and, if necessary, question each other's data.
- Openness about costs and activities often leads to new thinking.
- It is important to recognise anti-competition regulations and allow for reporting of commercially sensitive information to the commissioner only if needed.
- Proactively avoid the Alliance being seen as a cartel.

Principle 6 – Best person basis

f) To appoint and select key roles on a best person basis:

- People working in the Alliance are working for everyone. It should not matter which organisation they come from or who they receive their pay from.
- There must be a sense of 'leave your organisation at the door'.
- This provides the freedom to appoint or select the best people for the role, from any of the member organisations or externally.

Principle 7 – Values and behaviours

g) To act in accordance with the Alliance values and behaviours at all times:

- Each alliance creates its own set of values.
- These usually reflect the specific set of services or people the Alliance works with.
- As an alliance is forming, we advise an exercise to develop shared values.

Index

Printed in the United States
by Baker & Taylor Publisher Services

Printed in the United States
by Baker & Taylor Publisher Services